LITTLE
Luxuries
BY KNIT PICKS

Photography by Amy Cave

Printed in the United States of America

First Printing, 2017

ISBN 978-1-62767-150-7

Versa Press, Inc
800-447-7829

www.versapress.com

CONTENTS

NANCY SHAWL

by Renate Siebke

FINISHED MEASUREMENTS

22" at highest point x 65" wide across top edge

YARN

Knit Picks Alpaca Cloud Lace (100% Baby Alpaca; 440 yards/50g): Hugh 26770, 2 balls.

NEEDLES

US 4 (3.5mm) 24" or longer circular needles, or size to obtain gauge.

NOTIONS

Yarn Needle
Stitch Markers
Optional: Size 0.75 mm Crochet hook for placing beads or size small enough to fit through bead opening.
350 beads for the border of the flower chart in size 4 mm(6/0).

GAUGE

20 sts and 30 rows = 4" in Seed stitch, blocked. (Gauge for this project is approximate)

Nancy Shawl

Notes:

Nancy-Crescent is an extremely clever yet easily knit crescent-shaped shawl, that is sure to become your favorite accessory for almost any occasion! A combination of two panels, one in lace knitting, the other panel in Seed Stitch, come together in a unique way to create a curved slightly asymmetric triangle.

Once you have finished the set-up and completed the first pattern repeats, you will not even need to look at the written instructions or charts any more until you reach the border which introduces an easier lace stitch.

It is knitted asymmetrically, one half of the body features small flowers, which blend into the border with an optional picot-finish or elastic bind-off, the other half is bound off elastically or with an applied I-Cord.

You should weigh your yarn before you cast on and regularly, to make sure you do not run out of yarn. As a guideline, my percentage is given in some places.

Depending on how wide you want the border to be, I advise starting the incomplete pattern repeat before the actual border, when there is 25-35% of your yarn left. Depending on which border you want to knit, there are options for both a wide and a slim border. As there are different BO options, usage of yarn for BO varies. Make sure you have got enough yarn left for the chosen BO method.

The pattern helps keep you organized with one chart for set-up, including Seed Stitch Panel, Flower-Chart 1 (both charts worked once), Flower-Chart 2 (worked 9 or 10 times plus Rows 1-12 worked once more) and one of the Border Charts (worked once). It also contains fully written instructions. It includes instructions for modifications at the end as well as suggestions for optional bead placement. Read charts on RS rows (odd numbers) from right to left, and on WS rows (even numbers) from left to right.

Elastic Bind Off: K1, *K1, Sl the two sts on your RH needle back to LH needle and K2tog TBL; rep from * until all sts are BO.

Optional Picot Bind-off (if not used, work Elastic Bind Off instead): In the lace section only, K1, *K1, Sl the two sts on your RH needle back to LH needle and K2tog TBL, rep from * 7 times for a slim border, or 4 times for a wide border, the st on your RH needle should be the one lining up above st number 14 of Nancy Border Chart, the second K2tog of Row 13/17.
CO 1 st using a Knitted CO, BO the newly CO st. If you want your picots to be well centered you should now knit and subsequently BO the center st once again by placing the tip of your LH needle into this st (of Row 14/18), work picots according to instructions in the lace section until you reach the seed stitch section, work the Elastic Bind-off until all sts are BO.

Optional Applied I-cord Bind-off (for Seed Stitch Panel, if not used work Elastic Bind Off instead): This will be worked on the WS row after completing Row 9/11/13 or Row 13/15/17 of Flower-Chart 2: CO 2 sts. Working very loosely, *K 2 sts and slip the 3rd st K-wise. PU and K one more st from the edge of the shawl. 4

sts on right needle. Using left needle tip, pass the slipped st over the last knitted st, leaving you with 3 sts on your right needle. Sl these 3 sts back onto the left needle tip, or slide to the other end of the needle, P-wise. Do not tug on the working yarn to keep the sts very loose.
Repeat these steps from * until you reach one st before the marker, turn work, Sl 3 sts P-wise WYIF, P1, SM, BO one more st, finish the lace section of this WS row.
If you worked the I-Cord after Row 9/11/13 or 13/15/17, you will have to work the last st of Row 13 and/or 15 or 15 and/or 17 of the Border-Chart as Ssk, and then turn your work without knitting the last 2 sts (next RS row, 1 st), which belong to the Seed Stitch panel.

Bead (PB): Place beads, if you wish, according to instructions on Knit Picks website:
http://tutorials.knitpicks.com/wptutorials/knitting-with-beads-the-crochet-hook-method/
Place bead before you knit the st, if you do not want to use beads, just K (RS only).

Double Yarn Over (dyo): Wrap yarn over needle twice. 2 sts inc. On following rows, work the dyo sts as P1, K1.

DIRECTIONS
CO 4 sts. Turn and knit one row (RS).
Next Row (WS): P1, K2, P1.

Set Up
Work from Nancy Setup-Chart Rows 1-26 once, or written instructions below.
Row 1 (RS): K2, YO, K2. 5 sts.
Row 2 (WS): P3, PM, P2.
Row 3: K2, YO, SM, K1, YO, K2. 7 sts.
Row 4: P4, SM, P3.
Row 5: K2, YO, K1, YO, SM, K1, P1, YO, K2. 10 sts.
Row 6: P5, SM, P5.
Row 7: K1, Ssk, YO, K1, YO, K1 TBL, YO SM, Ssk, P1, dyo, K2. 13 sts.
Row 8: P3, K1, P2, SM, P7.
Row 9: K1, Ssk, YO, Ssk, K1, YO, K1 TBL, YO, SM, Ssk, K1, P1, dyo, K2. 15 sts.
Row 10: P3, K1, P1, K1, P1, SM, P8.
Row 11: K1, Ssk, YO, Ssk, K2, YO, K1 TBL, YO, SM, Ssk, P1, K1, P1, dyo, K2. 17 sts.
Row 12: P3, K1, P1, K1, P2, SM, P9.
Row 13: K1, Ssk, YO, Ssk, K3, YO, K1 TBL, YO, SM, Ssk, (K1, P1) twice, dyo, K2. 19 sts.
Row 14: P3, *K1, P1; rep from * 2x more, SM, P10.
Row 15: K1, Ssk, YO, Ssk, K4, YO, K1 TBL, YO, SM, Ssk, P1, (K1, P1) twice, dyo, K2. 21 sts.
Row 16: P3, *K1, P1; rep from * 2x more, P1, SM, P11.
Row 17: K1, Ssk, YO, Ssk, K5, YO, K1 TBL, YO, SM, Ssk, *K1, P1; rep from * 2x more, dyo, K2. 23 sts.
Row 18: P3, *K1, P1; rep from * 3x more, SM, P12.
Row 19: K1, Ssk, YO, Ssk, K6, YO, K1 TBL, YO, SM, Ssk, *P1, K1; rep from * 2x more, P1, dyo, K2. 25 sts.
Row 20: P3, *K1, P1; rep from * 3x more, P1, SM, P13.
Row 21: K1, Ssk, YO, Ssk, K7, YO, K1 TBL, YO, SM, Ssk, *K1, P1; rep from * 3x more, dyo, K2. 27 sts.

Row 22: P3, *K1, P1; rep from * 4x more, SM, P14.

Row 23: K1, Ssk, YO, Ssk, K8, YO, K1 TBL, YO, SM, Ssk, *P1, K1; rep from to last 3 sts, P1, dyo, K2. 29 sts.

Row 24: P3, K1, P1, *K1, P1; rep from to 3 sts before M, K1, P2, SM, P15.

Row 25: K1, Ssk, YO, Ssk, K9, YO, K1 TBL, YO, SM, Ssk, K1, *P1, K1; rep from * to last 3 sts, P1, dyo, K2. 31 sts.

Row 26: P3, *K1, P1; rep from to 4 sts before M, (K1, P1) twice, SM, P16.

Work Rows 1-26 once.

Flower Chart 1

Work from Nancy Flower-Chart 1 Rows 1-24 once (only sts for the lace section are charted, work Seed Stitch Panel including dyo's as established), or work from written instructions below.

Note: For the Seed Stitch Panel you will continue as established in the Setup-Chart by repeating instructions for Rows 23 to 26 of Nancy Setup-Chart.

Row 1 (RS): K1, Ssk, YO, Ssk, K3, K2tog, YO, K1, YO, Ssk, K2, YO, K1 TBL, YO, SM, work Seed Stitch Panel (Row 23 of Setup) as established in Setup-Chart. 2 sts inc.

Row 2 (WS): Work Seed Stitch Panel (Row 24 of Setup), SM, P17.

Row 3: K1, Ssk, YO, Ssk, K1, K2tog, YO, K1, PB, K1, YO, Ssk, K3, YO, K1 TBL, YO, SM, work Seed Stitch Panel (Row 25 of Setup). 2 sts inc.

Row 4: Work Seed Stitch Panel (Row 26 of Setup), SM, P18.

Row 5: K1, Ssk, YO, Ssk, K1, K2tog, YO, K1, YO, Ssk, K6, YO, K1 TBL, YO, SM, work Seed Stitch Panel. 2 sts inc.

Row 6 and all WS rows through Row 24: Work Seed Stitch Panel as established, SM, P to end.

Row 7: K1, Ssk, YO, Ssk, K6, K2tog, YO, K1, YO, Ssk, K2, YO, K1 TBL, YO, SM, work Seed Stitch Panel. 2 sts inc.

Row 9: K1, Ssk, YO, Ssk, K4, K2tog, YO, K1, PB, K1, YO, Ssk, K3, YO, K1 TBL, YO, SM, work Seed Stitch Panel. 2 sts inc

Row 11: K1, Ssk, YO, Ssk, K4, K2tog, YO, K1, YO, Ssk, K6, YO, K1 TBL, YO, SM, work Seed Stitch Panel. 2 sts inc.

Row 13: K1, Ssk, YO, Ssk, K9, K2tog, YO, K1, YO, Ssk, K2, YO, K1 TBL, YO, SM, work Seed Stitch Panel. 2 sts inc.

Row 15: K1, Ssk, YO, Ssk, K7, K2tog, YO, K1, PB, K1, YO, Ssk, K3, YO, K1 TBL, YO, SM, work Seed Stitch Panel. 2 sts inc.

Row 17: K1, Ssk, YO, Ssk, K7, K2tog, YO, K1, YO, Ssk, K6, YO, K1 TBL, YO, SM, work Seed Stitch Panel. 2 sts inc,

Row 19: K1, Ssk, YO, Ssk, K12, K2tog, YO, K1, YO, Ssk, K2, YO, K1 TBL, YO, SM, work Seed Stitch Panel. 2 sts inc.

Row 21: K1, Ssk, YO, Ssk, K10, K2tog, YO, K1, PB, K1, YO, Ssk, K3, YO, K1 TBL, YO, SM, work Seed Stitch Panel. 2 sts inc.

Row 23: K1, Ssk, YO, Ssk, K10, K2tog, YO, K1, YO, Ssk, K6, YO, K1 TBL, YO, SM, work Seed Stitch Panel. 2 sts inc.

Work Rows 1-24 once.

Flower Chart 2

Work from Nancy Flower-Chart 2 or written instructions, below, repeating Rows 1-24 a total of 9 (10) times, then rep Rows 1-12 once more. There should be 11 (12) flowers per row before starting the Border Chart.

Note: For the Seed Stitch Panel you will continue as established in the Nancy Setup-Chart by repeating instructions for Rows 23 to 26 of Setup Chart. Each pattern rep adds 24 sts, 12 sts per panel, and the last rep up to Row 12 adds 12 sts altogether, 6 per panel.

Row 1 (RS): K1, Ssk, YO, Ssk, K2 , *K1, K2tog, YO, K1, YO, Ssk, K6*, K1, K2tog, YO, K1, YO, Ssk, K2 , YO, K1 TBL, YO, SM, work Seed Stitch Panel as established. 2 sts inc.

Row 2 and all WS rows through Row 24: Work Seed Stitch Panel as established, SM, P to end.

Row 3: K1, Ssk, YO, Ssk, K1, *K2tog, YO, K1, PB, K1, YO, Ssk, K5*, K2tog, YO, K1, PB, K1, YO, Ssk, K3, YO, K1 TBL, YO, SM, work Seed Stitch Panel. 2 sts inc.

Row 5: K1, Ssk, YO, Ssk, *K1, K2tog, YO, K1, YO, Ssk, K6*, K1, K2tog, YO, K1, YO, Ssk, K6, YO, K1 TBL, YO, SM, work Seed Stitch Panel. 2 sts inc.

Row 7: K1, Ssk, YO, Ssk, K5, *K1, K2tog, YO, K1, YO, Ssk, K6*, K1, K2tog, YO, K1, YO, Ssk, K2 , YO, K1 TBL, YO, SM, work Seed Stitch Panel. 2 sts inc.

Row 9: K1, Ssk, YO, Ssk, K4, *K2tog, YO, K1, PB, K1, YO, Ssk, K5*, K2tog, YO, K1, PB, K1, YO, Ssk, K3, YO, K1 TBL, YO, SM, work Seed Stitch Panel. 2 sts inc.

Row 11: K1, Ssk, YO, Ssk, K3, *K1, K2tog, YO, K1, YO, Ssk, K6*, K1, K2tog, YO, K1, YO, Ssk, K6, YO, K1 TBL, YO, SM, work Seed Stitch Panel. 2 sts inc.

Row 13: K1, Ssk, YO, Ssk, K8, *K1, K2tog, YO, K1, YO, Ssk, K6*, K1, K2tog, YO, K1, YO, Ssk, K2 , YO, K1 TBL, YO, SM, work Seed Stitch Panel. 2 sts inc.

Row 15: K1, Ssk, YO, Ssk, K7, *K2tog, YO, K1, PB, K1, YO, Ssk, K5*, K2tog, YO, K1, PB, K1, YO, Ssk, K3, YO, K1 TBL, YO, SM, work Seed Stitch Panel. 2 sts inc.

Row 17: K1, Ssk, YO, Ssk, K6, *K1, K2tog, YO, K1, YO, Ssk, K6*, K1, K2tog, YO, K1, YO, Ssk, K6, YO, K1 TBL, YO, SM, work Seed Stitch Panel. 2 sts inc.

Row 19: K1, Ssk, YO, Ssk, K11, *K1, K2tog, YO, K1, YO, Ssk, K6*, K1, K2tog, YO, K1, YO, Ssk, K2 , YO, K1 TBL, YO, SM, work Seed Stitch Panel. 2 sts inc.

Row 21: K1, Ssk, YO, Ssk, K10, *K2tog, YO, K1, PB, K1, YO, Ssk, K5*, K2tog, YO, K1, PB, K1, YO, Ssk, K3, YO, K1 TBL, YO, SM, work Seed Stitch Panel. 2 sts inc.

Row 23: K1, Ssk, YO, Ssk, K9, *K1, K2tog, YO, K1, YO, Ssk, K6*, K1, K2tog, YO, K1, YO, Ssk, K6, YO, K1 TBL, YO, SM, work Seed Stitch Panel. 2 sts inc.

Border

For the border you have two options, work a Slim Border with 14 rows plus BO, or a Wide Border with 18 rows plus BO. If you did only 9 complete repeats of Flower-Chart 2, there should be enough yarn left for the wider border.

Slim Border Option

Please have a close look at the three different ways to finish the Seed Stitch Panel, as you may start binding off there as early as after Row 9. Also you have two options for the lace section, both worked in Row 15 or Row 19.

Note: Remember to work final rep of Rows 1-12 of Flower-Chart 2 in previous section before beginning Border.

Work from Border Chart 4, working Rows 1-14, or follow written directions, below.

Row 1 (RS): K1, Ssk, YO, Ssk, K9, K2tog, YO, K1, *YO, Ssk, K7, K2tog, YO, K1*, YO, Ssk, K2, YO, K1 TBL, YO, SM, Seed Stitch Panel.

Row 2 and all WS rows through Row 12: Work Seed Stitch Panel as established, SM, P to end.

Row 3: K1, (Ssk, YO) three times, Ssk, K1, (K2tog, YO) twice, K1, PB, *K1, (YO, Ssk) twice, K1, (K2tog, YO) twice, K1, PB *, K1, (YO, Ssk) twice, K1, YO, K1 TBL, YO, SM, work Seed Stitch Panel.

Row 5: K1, (Ssk, YO) three times, Sk2p, YO, K2tog, YO, K2tog, YO, K1, * (YO, Ssk) twice, YO, Sk2p, (YO, K2tog) twice, YO.

Row 7: K1, (Ssk, YO) twice, Ssk, K1, (K2tog, YO) twice, K1, PB*, K1, (YO, Ssk) twice, K1, K2tog, YO, K2tog, K1, YO, K1 TBL, YO, SM, work Seed Stitch Panel.

Row 9: K1, (Ssk, YO) twice, Sk2p, (YO, K2tog) twice, YO, K1, *(YO, Ssk) twice, YO, Sk2p, (YO, K2tog) twice, YO, K1*, (YO, Ssk) twice, YO, Sk2p, (YO, K2tog) twice, YO, K1, YO, K1 TBL, YO, SM, work Seed Stitch Panel, after this row is the first spot for working the Applied I-Cord Bind-off.

Row 11: K1, Ssk, YO, Ssk, K1, (K2tog, YO) twice, K1, PB, K1, (YO, Ssk) twice, K1, (K2tog, YO) twice, K1, PB*, K1, (YO, Ssk) twice, K1, (K2tog, YO) twice, K1, PB, K2, YO, K1 TBL, YO, SM, work Seed Stitch Panel, after this row is the second spot for working the Applied I-Cord Bind-off.

Row 13: K1, Ssk, YO, Sk2p, (YO, K2tog) twice, YO, K1, *(YO, Ssk) twice, YO, Sk2p, YO, (K2tog, YO) twice, K1*, (YO, Ssk) twice, YO, Sk2p, (YO, K2tog) twice, YO, K1, (YO, Ssk) twice, YO, K1 TBL, YO, SM, work Seed Stitch Panel, after this row is the last spot for working the Applied I-Cord Bind-off.

Row 14: Work Seed Stitch Panel as established, SM, k to end. Work Rows 1-14 once, then BO.

Wide Border Option

Please have a close look at the three different ways to finish the Seed Stitch Panel as you may start binding off there as early as after Row 13.

Note: Remember to work final rep of Rows 1-12 of Flower-Chart 2 in previous section before beginning Border.

Work Rows 1-18 of the Border Chart from either the Chart or written directions below, then move on to Bind off instructions.

Row 1: K1, Ssk, YO, Ssk, K9, K2tog, YO, K1, *YO, Ssk, K7, K2tog, YO, K1*, YO, Ssk, K2, YO, K1 TBL, YO, SM, Seed Stitch Panel.

Row 2 and all WS rows through Row 16: Work Seed Stitch Panel as established, SM, P to end.

Row 3: K1, (Ssk, YO) three times, Ssk, K1, (K2tog, YO) twice, K1, PB, *K1, (YO, Ssk) twice, K1, (K2tog, YO) twice, K1, PB*, K1, (YO, Ssk) twice, K1, YO, K1 TBL, YO, SM, work Seed Stitch Panel.

Row 5: K1, (Ssk, YO) three times, Sk2p, (YO, K2tog) twice, YO, K1, *(YO, Ssk) twice, YO, Sk2p, (YO, K2tog) twice, YO, K1*, (YO, Ssk) three times, YO, K2, YO, K1 TBL, YO, SM, work Seed Stitch Panel.

Row 7: K1, (Ssk, YO) twice, Ssk, K1, (K2tog, YO) twice, K1, PB, * K1, (YO, Ssk) twice, K1, (K2tog, YO) twice, K1, PB*, K1, (YO, Ssk) twice, K1, K2tog, YO, K2tog, K1, YO, K1 TBL, YO, SM, work Seed Stitch Panel.

Row 9: K1, (Ssk, YO) twice, Sk2p, (YO, K2tog) twice, YO, K1, *(YO, Ssk) twice, YO, Sk2p, (YO, K2tog) twice, YO, K1*, (YO, Ssk) twice, YO, Sk2p, (YO, K2tog) twice, YO, K1, YO, K1 TBL, YO, SM, work Seed Stitch Panel.

Row 11: K1, Ssk, YO, Ssk, K1, (K2tog, YO) twice, K1, PB, *K1, (YO, Ssk) twice, K1, (K2tog, YO) twice, K1, PB*, K1, (YO, Ssk) twice, K1, (K2tog, YO) twice, K1, PB, K2, YO, K1 TBL, YO, SM, work Seed

Stitch Panel.

Row 13: K1, Ssk, YO, Sk2p, (YO, K2tog) twice, YO, K1, *(YO, Ssk) twice, YO, Sk2p, (YO, K2tog) twice, YO, K1*, (YO, Ssk) twice, YO, Sk2p, (YO, K2tog) twice, YO, K1, (YO, Ssk) twice, YO, K1 TBL, YO, SM, work Seed Stitch Panel, after this row is the first spot for working the Applied I-Cord Bind-off.

Row 15: K1, Ssk, K1, (K2tog, YO) twice, K1, PB, * K1, (YO, Ssk) twice, K1, (K2tog, YO) twice, K1, PB*, K1, (YO, Ssk) twice, K1, (K2tog, YO) twice, K1, PB, K1, (YO, Ssk) twice, K1, YO, K1 TBL, YO, SM, work Seed Stitch Panel, after this row is the second spot for working the Applied I-Cord Bind-off.

Row 17: K1, Sk2p, (YO, K2tog) twice, YO, K1, *(YO, Ssk) twice, YO, Sk2p, (YO, K2tog) twice, YO, K1*, (YO, Ssk) twice, YO, Sk2p, YO, (K2tog, YO) twice, K1, (YO, Ssk) four times, YO, K1 TBL, YO, SM, work Seed Stitch Panel, after this row is the last spot for working the Applied I-Cord Bind-off.

Row 18: Work Seed Stitch Panel as established, SM, k to end. Work Rows 1-18 once, then BO.

Bind Off

Bind off using Elastic Bind Off, or place picots above sts 14/16/18 *26/28/30*38/40/42.

Finishing

Weave in ends, wash and block hard to diagram. If you worked picots, make sure to pin them out separately.

Legend

knit
RS: knit stitch
WS: purl stitch

ssk
Slip one stitch as if to knit, slip another stitch as if to knit. Insert left-hand needle into front of these 2 stitches and knit them together

yo
Yarn over

purl
RS: purl stitch
WS: knit stitch

No Stitch
Placeholder - No stitch made.

place bead

sl1 k2tog psso
RS: slip 1, k2tog, pass slip stitch over k2tog

bind off

k2tog
RS: Knit two stitches together as one stitch
WS: Purl 2 stitches together

pattern repeat

knit tbl
RS: Knit stitch through back loop
WS: Purl stitch through back loop

Set Up Chart

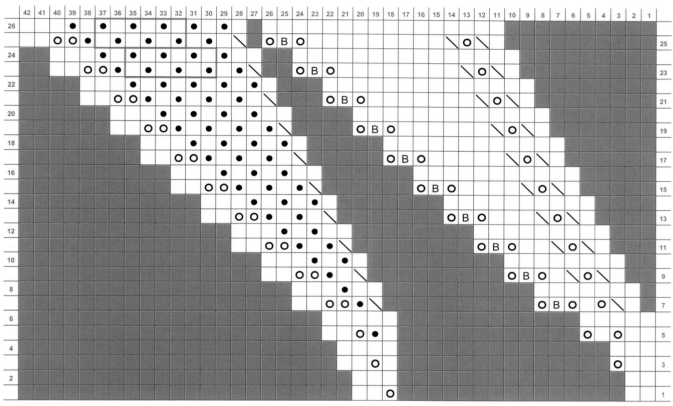

Chart 1

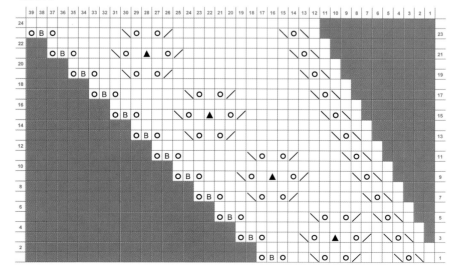

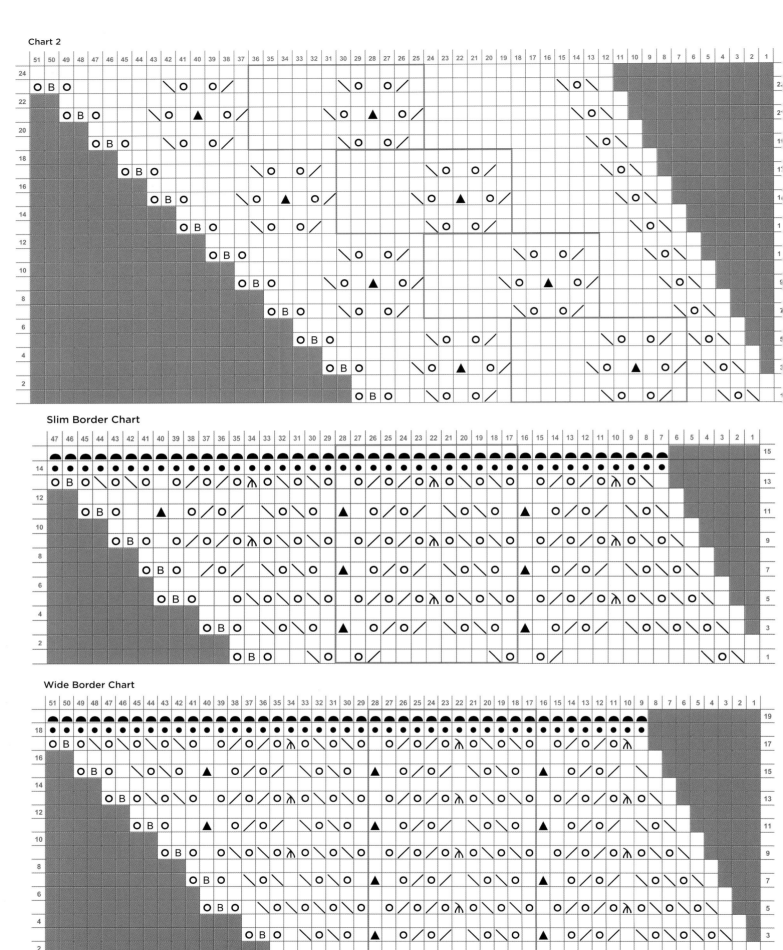

Chart 2

Slim Border Chart

Wide Border Chart

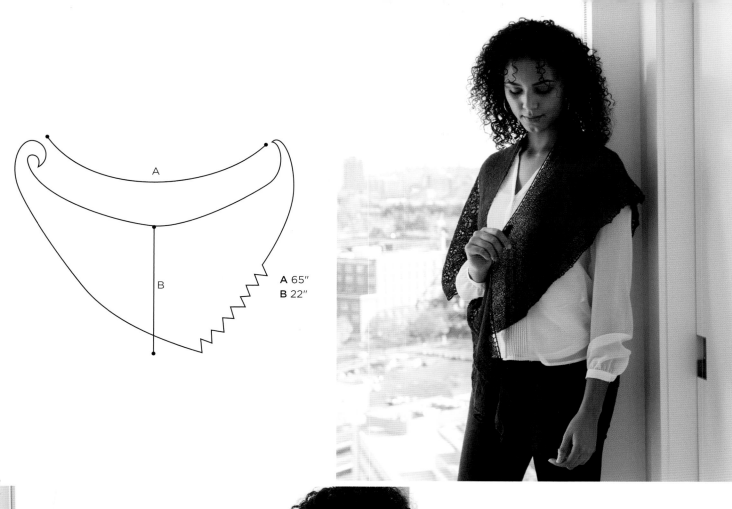

A 65"
B 22"

CURLY CABLE MITTENS

by Solène Le Roux

FINISHED MEASUREMENTS

6 (7, 8)" hand circumference, length is adjustable

YARN

Knit Picks Galileo (50% Merino Wool, 50% Viscose from Bamboo; 131 yards/50g): Dragonfly 26105, 2 balls

NEEDLES

US 5 (3.75mm) DPNs or long circular needle for Magic Loop technique, or size to obtain gauge

NOTIONS

Yarn Needle
Stitch Marker
Cable Needle
Scrap Yarn

GAUGE

24 sts and 27 rows = 4" over Hand Cable Pattern in the rnd, blocked

Curly Cable Mittens

Notes:

These mittens are knit from the cuff. The top of the hand is knit in a 3 stitch cable pattern repeat, and the palm in stockinette stitch. Both hands are different. The thumbs are separated using scrap yarn and feature a 4 stitch cable framed by purl stitches. You can try the mittens on as you knit them and adjust the length as desired.

Right Twist (1-1RC): Sl1 to CN, hold in back, K1, K1 from CN.
Left Twist (1-1LC): Sl1 to CN, hold in front, K1, K1 from CN.
Right Twist, Purl Background (1-1RPC): Sl1 to CN, hold in back, K1, P1 from CN.
Left Twist, Purl Background (1-1LPC): Sl1 to CN, hold in front, P1, K1 from CN.

Hand Cable Pattern (in the rnd over multiples of 3 sts)
Rnd 1: *1-1RC, P1; rep from *.
Rnd 2: *K2, P1; rep from *.
Rnd 3: *1-1LC, P1; rep from *
Rnd 4: *K2, P1; rep from *.

Thumb Cable Pattern (in the rnd over 6 sts)
Rnd 1: P1, 1-1RPC, 1-1LPC, P1.
Rnd 2: P1, K1, P2, K1, P1.
Rnd 3: P1, 1-1LPC, 1-1RPC, P1.
Rnd 4: P2, K2, P2.
Rnd 5: P2, 1-1RC, P2.
Rnd 6: P2, K2, P2.

Kitchener Stitch (grafting): For a tutorial on Kitchener St, see: http://tutorials.knitpicks.com/wptutorials/kitchener-stitch/

DIRECTIONS

Cuff (both hands)
Loosely CO 36 (42, 48) sts. PM and join to work in the rnd, being careful not to twist sts.
Rnd 1: *K1, P1; rep from * to end.
Repeat Rnd 1 until you reach 2.5".

Right Hand
Rnd 1: K6, P1, work Hand Cable Pattern 5 (6, 7) times, work Thumb Cable Pattern, K8 (11, 14).
Repeat Rnd 1 until you reach 6.5" from CO, or desired length before thumb separation.

Separate Thumb Rnd: K6, P1, work Hand Cable Pattern 5 (6, 7) times, with scrap yarn K6, Sl the 6 scrap yarn sts back to LH needle, with main yarn K to end.

Left Hand
Rnd 1: Work Thumb Cable Pattern, P1, work Hand Cable Pattern 5 (6, 7) times, K14 (17, 20).
Repeat Rnd 1 until you reach 6.5" from CO, or desired length before thumb separation.

Separate Thumb Rnd: With scrap yarn K6, Sl the 6 scrap yarn sts back to LH needle, with main yarn K6, P1, work Hand Cable Pattern 5 (6, 7) times, K to end.

Both Hands
Rnd 1: K6, P1, work Hand Cable Pattern 5 (6, 7) times, K to end.
Repeat Rnd 1 until you reach 10" from CO, or 1" less than desired length.

Decreases (both hands)
During the decreases, when there are not enough sts to work a full cable, knit the stitches instead.
Rnd 1: K3, K2tog, SSK, work 14 (17, 20) sts in Hand Cable Pattern, K2tog, SSK, K to end. 32 (38, 44) sts.
Rnd 2: K5, work 14 (17, 20) sts in Hand Cable Pattern, K to end.
Rnd 3: K2, K2tog, SSK, work 12 (15, 18) sts in Hand Cable Pattern, K2tog, SSK, K to end. 28 (34, 40) sts.
Rnd 4: K4, work 12 (15, 18) sts in Hand Cable Pattern, K to end.
Rnd 5: K1, K2tog, SSK, work 10 (13, 16) sts in Hand Cable Pattern, K2tog, SSK, K to end. 24 (30, 36) sts.
Rnd 6: K3, work 10 (13, 16) sts in Hand Cable Pattern, K to end.
Rnd 7: K2tog, SSK, work 8 (11, 14) sts in Hand Cable Pattern, K2tog, SSK, K to end. 20 (26, 32) sts.
Rearrange your sts as follow: K1, put following 10 (13, 16) sts on Needle 1, and remaining 10 (13, 16) sts on Needle 2. Graft the sts together using Kitchener Stitch.

Thumb (both hands)
Set-up Rnd: PU 6 sts under scrap yarn, PU 1 st on the side, PU 6 sts over scrap yarn, PU 1 sts on the side. 14 sts.
Remove scrap yarn, PM and join in the rnd.

Rnd 1: Work Thumb Cable Pattern, K to end.
Rep Rnd 1 until your thumb reaches 2", or 0.5" less than desired length, ending with Rnd 6 of Thumb Cable Pattern.

Thumb Decreases
Rnd 1: K2tog to end of rnd. 7 sts.
Rnd 2: K1, K2tog, K to end. 6 sts.
Rearrange your sts as follow: Put the first 3 sts on Needle 1, the last 3 sts on Needle 2 and graft them together using Kitchener Stitch.

Finishing
Weave in ends, wash and block.

Hand Cable

3	2	1	
●			4
●	╲╱	╲╱	3
●			2
●	╱╲	╱╲	1

Thumb Cable

6	5	4	3	2	1	
●	●			●	●	6
●	●	╲╱	╲╱	●	●	5
●	●			●	●	4
●	╱	╱╲	╲●		●	3
●		●	●		●	2
●	╱╲	╲●	╱	╱╲	●	1

Legend

	Right Twist
╲╱ ╲╱	sl1 to CN, hold in back. k1, k1 from CN

	Left Twist
╱╲ ╱╲	sl1 to CN, hold in front. k1, k1 from CN

	purl
●	purl stitch

	knit
□	knit stitch

	Right Twist, purl bg
╱ ╲	sl1 to CN, hold in back. k1, p1 from CN

	Left Twist, purl bg
╲ ╱	sl1 to CN, hold in front. p1. k1 from CN

HONEYCOMB HAT

by Deepika

FINISHED MEASUREMENTS
20" circumference, 8.5" high, to fit head 23" around

YARN
Knit Picks Paragon (50% Fine Merino , 25% Baby Alpaca, 25% Mulberry Silk; 123 yards/50g): Turmeric 26971 - 2 balls

NEEDLES
US 4 (3.50mm) 16" circular needles and a set of DPNs, or size to obtain gauge
US 3 (3.25mm) 16" circular needles, or one size smaller than needle to obtain gauge

NOTIONS
Yarn Needle
Stitch Markers
Cable Needle

GAUGE
36 sts and 32 rows = 4" in Honeycomb Cable Pattern on larger needle in the rnd, blocked

Honeycomb Hat

Notes:

This hat is worked from the bottom up, beginning with a ribbed brim. After knitting the brim, stitches are increased for the body of hat and the needle size is changed before beginning the cable pattern. It's a quick knit with an engaging cable pattern with a unique lacy look, worked bottom up, entirely in rounds.

If working from the charts, follow all chart rows from right to left, reading them as RS rows. Rep chart rows 15 times across the rnd.

C1 over 3 Right P: Sl 3 to CN and hold to back; K1, P3 from CN.
C1 over 3 Left P: Sl 1 to CN and hold to front; P3, K1 from CN.

DIRECTIONS

Using smaller sized needle loosely CO 120 sts. PM to indicate the beginning of the rnd. Join to begin working in the rnd, being careful not to twist sts.

Rnds 1-12: *K1, P1; rep from * - to the end of the rnd.
Increase Rnd: *K(kfb)*; rep from * to* -end of rnd. -(180 sts.)
Switch to larger sized circular needle and knit one rnd.

Honeycomb Cable Pattern.(Cable Chart A)

Rnd 1,2: *K3, P6, K3; rep from * to end of rnd.
Rnd 3: *K2, C1 over 3 left P, C1 over 3 right P, K2; rep from * to end of rnd.
Rnd 4: *(K2, P3)twice, K2; rep from * to end of rnd.
Rnd 5: *K1, C1 over 3 left P, K2, C1 over 3 right P, K1; rep from * to end of rnd.
Rnd 6: *K1, P3, K4, P3, K1; rep from * to end of rnd.
Rnd 7: *C1 over 3 left P, K4, C1 over 3 right P; rep from * to end of rnd.
Rnd 8, 9, 10: *P3, K6, P3; rep from * to end of round.
Rnd 11: *C1 over 3 right P, K4, C1 over 3 left P; rep from * to end of rnd.
Rnd 12: Rep rnd 6.
Rnd 13: *K1, C1 over 3 right P, K2, C1 over 3 left P, K1; rep from * to end of rnd.
Rnd 14: Rep rnd 4.
Rnd 15: *K2, C1 over 3 right P, C1 over 3 left P, K2; rep from * to end of rnd.
Rnd 16: Rep rnd 1.
Repeat Rnds 1-16 for pattern.

Work rep of rnds 1 to 16 of Honeycomb Cable Pattern 3 times or until piece is about 7" long measured from CO edge, ending at 16th rnd.

Decreases: (Chart B)

If using a 16" circular, change to DPNs when sts no longer fit comfortably on the needle.
Rnd 1,2: *K3, P6, K3; rep from * to end of rnd.
Rnd 3: *K1, K2tog, P6, SSK, K1; rep from * to end of rnd. 150 sts.
Rnd 4: *K2, P2tog, P2, P2tog, K2; rep from * to end of rnd. 120 sts.
Rnd 5: *K2tog, P1, P2tog, P1, SSK; rep from * to end of rnd. 75 sts
Rnd 6: *K1, P3tog, K1; rep from * to end of rnd. 45 sts.

Remove beginning of rnd M, K1, replace beginning of rnd M at this new position.
Rnd 7: *P1, K2; rep from * to end of rnd.
Rnd 8: *P1, K2tog; rep from * to end of rnd. 30 sts.
Rnd 9: Knit to end of rnd.
Rnd 10: *K2tog; rep from * to end of rnd. 15 sts .

Finishing

Cut yarn, leaving a tail of 6 to 8". Using yarn needle, draw yarn through remaining 15 sts. and pull tight and weave in all ends on WS, block to Finished Measurements.

Chart A

12	11	10	9	8	7	6	5	4	3	2	1	
			•	•	•	•	•	•				16
				╱	·	·	╲					15
			•	•	•			•	•	•		14
		╱			·			·			╲	13
		•	•	•					•	•	•	12
		╱			·			·			╲	11
•	•	•							•	•	•	10
•	•	•							•	•	•	9
•	•	•							•	•	•	8
·			╱					╲			·	7
		•	•	•			•	•	•			6
	·			╱			╲			·		5
			•	•	•	•	•	•				4
				╱			╲					3
			•	•	•	•	•	•				2
			•	•	•	•	•	•				1

Chart B

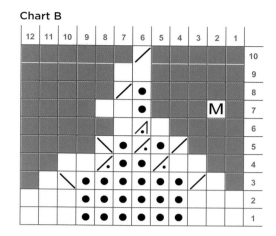

12	11	10	9	8	7	6	5	4	3	2	1	
						╱						10
												9
					╱	•						8
						•		M				7
					╱							6
				╱	•	·	•	╲				5
			╱	•	•	•	•	╲				4
		╱	•	•	•	•	•	•	╲			3
			•	•	•	•	•	•				2
				•	•	•	•	•				1

Legend

☐	**knit**	knit stitch
•	**purl**	purl stitch
⧄	**c1 over 3 left P**	sl 1 to CN, hold in front. p3, k1 from CN
⧅	**c1 over 3 right P**	sl 3 to CN, hold in back. k1, p3 from CN

╱·	**p2tog**	Purl 2 stitches together
╱	**p3tog**	Purl three stitches together as one
M	**Beginning of round marker**	Remove beginng of rnd M, k1, replace BOR marker at this new position

■	**No Stitch**	Placeholder - No stitch made.
╱	**k2tog**	Knit two stitches together as one stitch
╲	**ssk**	Slip one stitch as if to knit, slip another stitch as if to knit. Insert left-hand needle into front of these 2 stitches and knit them together

OBLIQUE CABLED MITTS

by Emily Kintigh

FINISHED MEASUREMENTS

7 (7.5, 8)" hand circumference, 3.75 (4.25, 4.75)" long without cuffs

YARN

Knit Picks Gloss Fingering (70% Merino Wool, 30% Silk; 220 yards/50g): Bordeaux 24610, 1 hank

NEEDLES

US 2 (2.75mm) straight needles, or size to obtain gauge
US 1 (2.25mm) DPNs, or one size below gauge needle

NOTIONS

Yarn Needle
Stitch Markers
Cable needle

GAUGE

32 sts and 40 rows = 4" St st on larger needles, blocked

Oblique Cabled Mitts

Notes:

The main part of the mitt is worked diagonally. The mitts and thumbs are worked flat, separately and then sewn together. Stitches are then picked up for the cuff and upper edge of the mitts, which are worked in the round.

Many of the increases are closed yarnover increases. A yarnover is worked on a right side row and then twisted on the following wrong side row. Some of the wrong side increases are KBFs instead of KFBs in order to increase and twist the yarnover from the previous row. To work this increase, knit into the back of the stitch first and then the front.

Right Twist (RT)
Skip the first st, K into the 2nd st, then knit skipped st. Sl both sts from needle.

Left Twist (LT)
Sl1 to CN, hold in front. K1, K1 from CN.

Right Twist, purl (RT PB)
Sl1 to CN, hold in back. K1, P1 from CN.

Left Twist, purl (LT PB)
Sl1 to CN, hold in front. P1, K1 from CN.

Knit back and front (KBF)
K into the back and then the front of the st.

DIRECTIONS
Right Hand Mitt
Beginning Shaping

With larger needles, CO 4 sts.
Row 1(WS): KFB, P2, KFB. 6 sts.
Row 2: P1, YO, P1, LT, P1, YO, P1. 8 sts.
Row 3: K1, Ktbl, K1, P2, K1, KBF, K1. 9 sts.
Row 4: P1, YO, P2, RT PB, LT PB, P1, YO, P1. 11 sts.
Row 5: K1, Ktbl, K1, P1, K2, P1, K2, KBF, K1. 12 sts.
Row 6: P1, YO, P3, RT PB, P2, LT PB, P1, YO, P1. 14 sts.
Row 7: K1, Ktbl, K1, P1, K4, P1, K3, KBF, K1. 15 sts.
Row 8: P1, YO, P4, RT, P4, LT, P1, YO, P1. 17 sts.
Row 9: K1, Ktbl, K1, (P2, K4) twice, KBF, K1. 18 sts.
Row 10: P1, YO, P3, (P2, RT PB, LT PB) twice, P1, YO, P1. 20 sts.
Row 11: K1, Ktbl, K1, P1, (K2, P1) three times, K5, KBF, K1. 21 sts.
Row 12: P1, YO, P7, K1, P2, LT PB, RT PB, P2, K1, P2, YO, P1. 23 sts.
Row 13: K1, Ktbl, PM, K2, P1, K3, P2, K3, P1, K2, PM, K5, KBF, K1. 24 sts.

Main Mitt

Row 1: P1, YO, P to first marker, work the Cable Chart beginning with Row 1 between markers, P to last st, YO, P1. 26 sts.
Row 2: K1, Ktbl, K to first marker, work the next row of the Cable Chart between markers, K to last 2 sts, KBF, K1. 27 sts.

Repeat Rows 1-2 another 4 (5, 6) times, continuing to work from the Cable Chart between the markers. 39 (42, 45) sts.

Next Row: P1, P2tog, P to first marker, work the Cable Chart continuing with Row 11 (13, 15) between markers, P to last st, YO, P1.

Next Row: K1, Ktbl, K to first marker, work the next row of the Cable Chart between markers, K to end.

Repeat last two rows, continuing to work from the Cable Chart between the markers. Work 30 (34, 38) more rows of Cable Chart, removing markers on last row and ending with Row 2 (8, 14) of chart.

Transition out of Cable and Final Shaping

For 7" Size:
Row 1: P1, P2tog, P2, (LT PB, RT PB) twice, P25, YO, P1.
Row 2: K1, Ktbl, K26, P2, K2, P2, K5.
Row 3: P1, P2tog, P2, RT, P2, LT, P27, YO, P1.
Row 4: K1, Ktbl, K27, P2, K2, P2, K4.
Row 5: P1, P2tog, (RT PB, LT PB) twice, P27, YO, P1.
Row 6: K1, Ktbl, K27, P1, K2, P2, K2, P1, K2.
Row 7: P1, P2tog, P2, LT, P2, LT PB, P25, P2tog, P1. 37 sts.
Row 8: K1, K2tog, K24, P1, K3, P2, K4. 36 sts.
Row 9: P1, P2tog, RT PB, LT PB, P2, K1, P23, P2tog, P1. 34 sts.
Row 10: K1, K2tog, K22, (P1, K2) three times. 33 sts.
Row 11: P1, P2tog, P2, LT PB, RT PB, P21, P2tog, P1. 31 sts.
Row 12: K1, K2tog, K21, P2, K5. 30 sts.
Row 13: P1, P2tog, P2, LT, P20, P2tog, P1. 28 sts.
Row 14: K1, K2tog, K19, P2, K4. 27 sts.
Row 15: P1, P2tog, RT PB, LT PB, P17, P2tog, P1. 25 sts.
Row 16: K1, K2tog, K16, (P1, K2) twice. 24 sts.
Row 17: P1, P2tog, P2, K1, P15, P2tog, P1. 22 sts.
Row 18: K1, K2tog, K14, P1, K4. 21 sts.
Row 19: P1, P2tog, RT PB, P13, P2tog, P1. 19 sts.
Row 20: K1, K2tog, K13, P1, K2. 18 sts.
Row 21: P1, P2tog, P to last 3 sts, P2tog, P1. 16 sts.
Row 22: K1, K2tog, K to end. 15 sts.
Rows 23-30: Repeat Rows 21-22 four more times. 3 sts.
Pull yarn through rem sts. Wash and block to final measurements.

For 7.5" Size:
Row 1: P1, P2tog, P1, RT PB, P2, LT, P2, LT PB, P27, YO, P1.
Row 2: K1, Ktbl, K27, P1, K3, P2, K3, P1, K3.
Row 3: P1, P2tog, K1, P2, RT PB, LT PB, P2, K1, P28, YO, P1.
Row 4: K1, Ktbl, K28, P1, (K2, P1) three times, K2.
Row 5: P1, P2tog, P1, RT PB, P2, LT PB, RT PB, P27, P2tog, P1. 40 sts.
Row 6: K1, K2tog, K27, P2, K4, P1, K3. 39 sts.
Row 7: P1, P2tog, K1, P4, LT, P26, P2tog, P1. 37 sts.
Row 8: K1, K2tog, K25, P2, K4, P1, K2. 36 sts.
Row 9: P1, P2tog, P3, RT PB, LT PB, P23, P2tog, P1. 34 sts.
Row 10: K1, K2tog, K22, P1, K2, P1, K5. 33 sts.
Row 11: P1, P2tog, P1, RT PB, P2, K1, P21, P2tog, P1. 31 sts.
Row 12: K1, K2tog, K20, (P1, K3) twice. 30 sts.
Row 13: P1, P2tog, K1, P2, RT PB, P19, P2tog, P1. 28 sts.
Row 14: K1, K2tog, K19, (P1, K2) twice. 27 sts.
Row 15: P1, P2tog, P1, RT PB, P18, P2tog, P1. 25 sts.
Row 16: K1, K2tog, K18, P1, K3. 24 sts.
Row 17: P1, P2tog, K1, P17, P2tog, P1. 22 sts.
Row 18: K1, K2tog, K16, P1, K2. 21 sts.
Row 19: P1, P2tog, P to last 3 sts, P2tog, P1. 19 sts.
Row 20: K1, K2tog, K to end. 18 sts.
Rows 21-30: Repeat Rows 19-20 five more times. 3 sts.
Pull yarn through rem sts. Wash and block to final measurements.

For 8" Size:

Row 1: P1, P2tog, P2, RT, P4, LT, P31, YO, P1.

Row 2: K1, Ktbl, K31, (P2, K4) twice.

Row 3: P1, P2tog, (RT PB, LT PB, P2) twice, P27, P2tog, P1. 43 sts.

Row 4: K1, K2tog, K28, (P1, K2) four times. 42 sts.

Row 5: P1, P2tog, P2, LT PB, RT PB, P2, K1, P27, P2tog, P1. 40 sts.

Row 6: K1, K2tog, K26, P1, K3, P2, K5. 39 sts.

Row 7: P1, P2tog, P2, RT, P2, RT PB, P25, P2tog, P1. 37 sts.

Row 8: K1, K2tog, K25, P1, K2, P2, K4. 36 sts.

Row 9: P1, P2tog, RT PB, LT PB, RT PB, P24, P2tog, P1. 34 sts.

Row 10: K1, K2tog, K24, P2, K2, P1, K2. 33 sts.

Row 11: P1, P2tog, P2, LT, P23, P2tog, P1. 31 sts.

Row 12: K1, K2tog, K22, P2, K4. 30 sts.

Row 13: P1, P2tog, RT PB, LT PB, P20, P2tog, P1. 28 sts.

Row 14: K1, K2tog, K19, (P1, K2) twice. 27 sts.

Row 15: P1, P2tog, P2, LT PB, P17, P2tog, P1. 25 sts.

Row 16: K1, K2tog, K16, P1, K5. 24 sts.

Row 17: P1, P2tog, P2, K1, P15, P2tog, P1. 22 sts.

Row 18: K1, K2tog, K14, P1, K4. 21 sts.

Row 19: P1, P2tog, RT PB, P13, P2tog, P1. 19 sts.

Row 20: K1, K2tog, K13, P1, K2. 18 sts.

Row 21: P1, P2tog, P to last 3 sts, P2tog, P1. 16 sts.

Row 22: K1, K2tog, K to end. 15 sts.

Rows 23-30: Repeat Rows 21-22 four more times. 3 sts.

Pull yarn through rem sts. Wash and block to final measurements.

Left Hand Mitt

Beginning Shaping

With larger needles, CO 4 sts.

Row 1(WS): KFB, P2, KFB. 6 sts.

Row 2: P1, YO, P1, LT, P1, YO, P1. 8 sts.

Row 3: K1, KBF, K1, P2, K1, Ktbl, K1. 9 sts.

Row 4: P1, YO, P1, RT PB, LT PB, P2, YO, P1. 11 sts.

Row 5: K1, KBF, (K2, P1) twice, K1, Ktbl, K1. 12 sts.

Row 6: P1, YO, P1, RT PB, P2, LT PB, P3, YO, P1. 14 sts.

Row 7: K1, KBF, K3, P1, K4, P1, K1, Ktbl, K1. 15 sts.

Row 8: P1, YO, P1, RT, P4, LT, P4, YO, P1. 17 sts.

Row 9: K1, KBF, (K4, P2) twice, K1, Ktbl, K1. 18 sts.

Row 10: P1, YO, P1, (RT PB, LT PB, P2) twice, P3, YO, P1. 20 sts.

Row 11: K1, KBF, K5, P1, (K2, P1) three times, K1, Ktbl, K1. 21 sts.

Row 12: P1, YO, P2, K1, P2, LT PB, RT PB, P2, K1, P7, YO, P1. 23 sts.

Row 13: K1, KBF, K5, PM, K2, P1, K3, P2, K3, P1, K2, PM, Ktbl, K1. 24 sts.

Main Mitt

Row 1: P1, YO, P to first marker, work the Cable Chart beginning with Row 1 between markers, P to last st, YO, P1. 26 sts.

Row 2: K1, KBF, K to first marker, work the next row of Cable Chart between markers, K to last two sts, Ktbl, K1. 27 sts.

Repeat Rows 1-2 another 4 (5, 6) times, continuing to work from the Cable Chart between the markers. 39 (42, 45) sts.

Next Row: P1, YO, P to first marker, work the Cable Chart continuing with Row 11 (13, 15) between markers, P to last 3 sts, SSP, P1.

Next Row: K to first marker, work the next row of the Cable Chart between markers, K to last 2 sts, Ktbl, K1.

Repeat last two rows, continuing to work from the Cable Chart between the markers. Work 30 (34, 38) more rows of Cable Chart, removing markers on last row and ending with Row 2 (8, 14) of chart.

Transition out of Cable and Final Shaping

For 7" Size:

Row 1: P1, YO, P25, (LT PB, RT PB) twice, P2, SSP, P1.

Row 2: K5, P2, K2, P2, K26, Ktbl, K1.

Row 3: P1, YO, P27, RT, P2, LT, P2, SSP, P1.

Row 4: K4, P2, K2, P2, K27, Ktbl, K1.

Row 5: P1, YO, P27, (RT PB, LT PB) twice, SSP, P1.

Row 6: K2, P1, K2, P2, K2, P1, K27, Ktbl, K1.

Row 7: P1, SSP, P25, RT PB, P2, LT, P2, SSP, P1. 37 sts.

Row 8: K4, P2, K3, P1, K24, SSK, K1. 36 sts.

Row 9: P1, SSP, P23, K1, P2, RT PB, LT PB, SSP, P1. 34 sts.

Row 10: (K2, P1) three times, K22, SSK, K1. 33 sts.

Row 11: P1, SSP, P21, LT PB, RT PB, P2, SSP, P1. 31 sts.

Row 12: K5, P2, K21, SSK, K1. 30 sts.

Row 13: P1, SSP, P20, RT, P2, SSP, P1. 28 sts.

Row 14: K4, P2, K19, SSK, K1. 27 sts.

Row 15: P1, SSP, P17, RT PB, LT PB, SSP, P1. 25 sts.

Row 16: (K2, P1) twice, K16, SSK, K1. 24 sts.

Row 17: P1, SSP, P15, K1, P2, SSP, P1. 22 sts.

Row 18: K4, P1, K14, SSK, K1. 21 sts.

Row 19: P1, SSP, P13, LT PB, SSP, P1. 19 sts.

Row 20: K2, P1, K13, SSK, K1. 18 sts.

Row 21: P1, SSP, P to last 3 sts, SSP, P1. 16 sts.

Row 22: K to last 3 sts, SSK, K1. 15 sts.

Rows 23-30: Repeat Rows 21-22 four more times. 3 sts.

Pull yarn through rem sts. Wash and block to final measurements.

For 7.5" Size:

Row 1: P1, YO, P27, RT PB, P2, LT, P2, LT PB, P1, SSP, P1.

Row 2: K3, P1, K3, P2, K3, P1, K27, Ktbl, K1.

Row 3: P1, YO, P28, K1, P2, RT PB, LT PB, P2, K1, SSP, P1.

Row 4: K2, (P1, K2) three times, P1, K28, Ktbl, K1.

Row 5: P1, SSP, P27, LT PB, RT PB, P2, LT PB, P1, SSP, P1. 40 sts.

Row 6: K3, P1, K4, P2, K27, SSK, K1. 39 sts.

Row 7: P1, SSP, P26, RT, P4, K1, SSP, P1. 37 sts.

Row 8: K2, P1, K4, P2, K25, SSK, K1. 36 sts.

Row 9: P1, SSP, P23, RT PB, LT PB, P3, SSP, P1. 34 sts.

Row 10: K5, P1, K2, P1, K22, SSK, K1. 33 sts.

Row 11: P1, SSP, P21, K1, P2, LT PB, P1, SSP, P1. 31 sts.

Row 12: (K3, P1) twice, K20, SSK, K1. 30 sts.

Row 13: P1, SSP, P19, LT PB, P2, K1, SSP, P1. 28 sts.

Row 14: (K2, P1) twice, K19, SSK, K1. 27 sts.

Row 15: P1, SSP, P18, LT PB, P1, SSP, P1. 25 sts.

Row 16: K3, P1, K18, SSK, K1. 24 sts.

Row 17: P1, SSP, P17, K1, SSP, P1. 22 sts.

Row 18: K2, P1, K16, SSK, K1. 21 sts.

Row 19: P1, SSP, P to last 3 sts, SSP, P1. 19 sts.

Row 20: K to last 3 sts, SSK, K1. 18 sts.

Rows 21-30: Repeat Rows 19-20 five more times. 3 sts.

Pull yarn through rem sts. Wash and block to final measurements.

For 8" Size:

Row 1: P1, YO, P31, RT, P4, LT, P2, SSP, P1.

Row 2: (K4, P2) twice, K31, Ktbl, K1.

Row 3: P1, SSP, P27, (P2, RT PB, LT PB) twice, SSP, P1. 43 sts.

Row 4: (K2, P1) four times, K28, SSK, K1. 42 sts.

Row 5: P1, SSP, P27, K1, P2, LT PB, RT PB, P2, SSP, P1. 40 sts.

Row 6: K5, P2, K3, P1, K26, SSK, K1. 39 sts.

Row 7: P1, SSP, P25, LT PB, P2, RT, P2, SSP, P1. 37 sts.

Row 8: K4, P2, K2, P1, K25, SSK, K1. 36 sts.

Row 9: P1, SSP, P24, LT PB, RT PB, LT PB, SSP, P1. 34 sts.

Row 10: K2, P1, K2, P2, K24, SSK, K1. 33 sts.

Row 11: P1, SSP, P23, RT, P2, SSP, P1. 31 sts.

Row 12: K4, P2, K22, SSK, K1. 30 sts.

Row 13: P1, SSP, P20, RT PB, LT PB, SSP, P1. 28 sts.

Row 14: (K2, P1) twice, K19, SSK, K1. 27 sts.

Row 15: P1, SSP, P17, RT PB, P2, SSP, P1. 25 sts.

Row 16: K5, P1, K16, SSK, K1. 24 sts.

Row 17: P1, SSP, P15, K1, P2, SSP, P1. 22 sts.

Row 18: K4, P1, K14, SSK, K1. 21 sts.

Row 19: P1, SSP, P13, LT PB, SSP, P1. 19 sts.

Row 20: K2, P1, K13, SSK, K1. 18 sts.

Row 21: P1, SSP, P to last 3 sts, SSP, P1. 16 sts.

Row 22: K to last 3 sts, SSK, K1. 15 sts.

Rows 23-30: Repeat Rows 21-22 four more times. 3 sts.

Pull yarn through rem sts. Wash and block to final measurements.

Thumb (Make two)

Gusset Increases

With larger needles, CO 4 sts.

Row 1(WS): K to end.

Row 2: P1, PFB twice, P1. 6 sts.

Row 3: K to end.

Row 4: P1, PFB, P to last 2 sts, PFB, P1. 8 sts.

Repeat Rows 3-4 another 3 (4, 5) times. 14 (16, 18) sts.

Next Row: Repeat Row 3.

Next Row: P to end.

Next Row: Repeat Row 3.

Next Row: Repeat Row 4.

Repeat last four rows twice more. 20 (22, 24) sts.

Main Thumb

Row 1: K to end.

Row 2: P to end.

Repeat Rows 1-2 another 0 (1, 2) times, then Row 1 once more. Switch to smaller needles.

For 7" and 8" sizes:

Next Row: K1, (K2, P2) to last 3 sts, K3.

Next Row: P1, (P2, K2) to last 3 sts, P3.

Repeat last two Rows once more.

BO all sts.

For 7.5" size:

Next Row: (K2, P2) to last 2 sts, K2.

Next Row: (P2, K2) to last 2 sts, P2.

Repeat last two Rows once more.

BO all sts.

Finishing:

Sew up the side of the thumb from the BO edge down to the last increase from the gusset using mattress stitch seaming. Sew the sides of the Main Mitt together, sewing the thumb approximately .75 (1, 1.25)" from top edge of mitt.

Cuffs

Complete finishing for the main mitt and thumb before working the cuff.

Bottom Cuff

With smaller needles, pick up 56 (60, 64) sts around the bottom of the mitt. Join in the rnd being careful not to twist the sts.

Rnd 1: (K2, P2) to end.

Repeat Rnd 1 until cuff measures 2 (2.25, 2.75)". Loosely BO all sts.

Top Cuff

With smaller needles, pick up 56 (60, 64) sts around the top of the mitt. Join in the rnd being careful not to twist the sts.

Rnd 1: (K2, P2) to end.

Repeat Rnd 1 until cuff measures .75". Loosely BO all sts.

Repeat for second mitt.

Finishing

Weave in ends, block again if desired.

Cable Chart

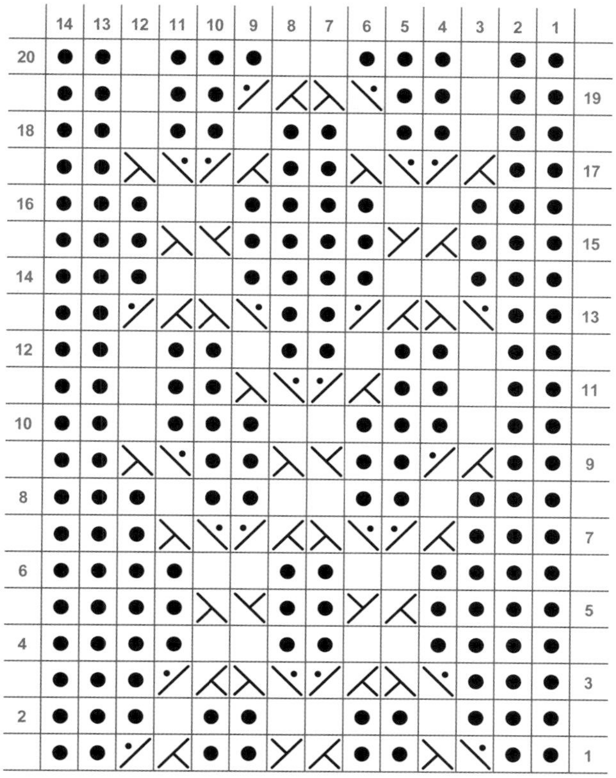

14 13 12 11 10 9 8 7 6 5 4 3 2 1
20
19
18
17
16
15
14
13
12
11
10
9
8
7
6
5
4
3
2
1

Legend

purl
RS: purl stitch
WS: knit stitch

Left Twist, purl bg
sl1 to CN, hold in front. p1. k1 from CN

Right Twist
Skip the first stitch, knit into 2nd stitch, then knit skipped stitch. Slip both stitches from needle together

Right Twist, purl bg
sl1 to CN, hold in back. k1, p1 from CN

knit
RS: knit stitch
WS: purl stitch

Left Twist
sl1 to CN, hold in front. k1, k1 from CN

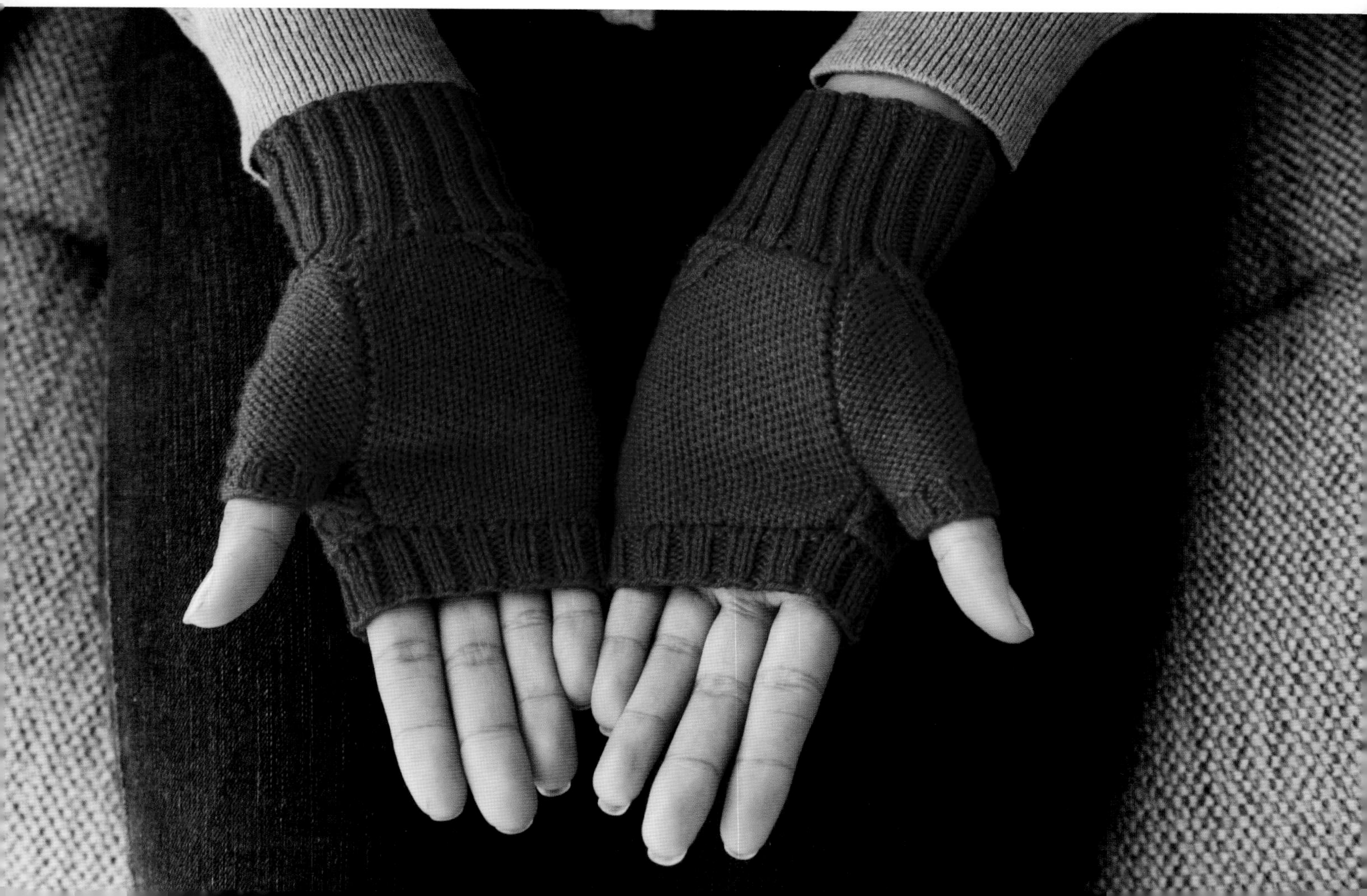

ISABEL COWL

by Trelly Hernández

FINISHED MEASUREMENTS
19" circumference x 11.25" high

YARN
Knit Picks Capretta (80% Fine Merino Wool, 10% Cashmere, 10% nylon; 230 yards/50g): Wine 25946, 2 balls

NEEDLES
US 4 (3.5 mm) 24" circular needles, or size to obtain gauge

NOTIONS
Yarn Needle
Stitch Marker

GAUGE
24 sts and 32 rows = 4" in Ribbing Pattern in the rnd, blocked.
32 sts and 33 rows = 4" over Chart 1 in the rnd, blocked

Isabel Cowl

Notes:

This cowl includes an easy lace pattern. Repeat each round of Chart 1 nineteen times in total, reading the chart from right to left.

Ribbing Pattern (worked in the rnd over an even number of sts)
All Rnds: *K1 tbl, p1; rep from * to end of rnd.

Sl2, K1, P2SSO: *Sl 2 sts K-wise, K1, pass 2 Sl sts over. 2 sts dec.

DIRECTIONS

Using the Long Tail Cast On, CO 152 sts, PM and join in the rnd being careful not to twist your sts.

Work Ribbing Pattern for 6 rnds.
Work Rnds 1-26 of Chart 1 three times in total.
Work Ribbing Pattern for 6 rnds.

Finishing

BO all sts, weave in ends, wash and block.

Chart 1

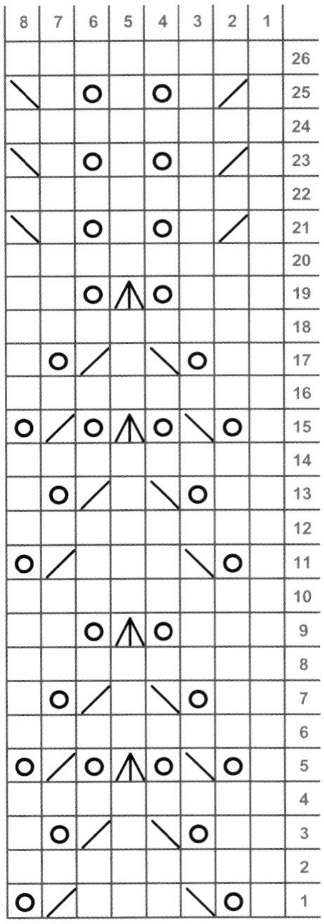

Legend

	knit	knit stitch
O	yo	Yarn Over
ssk		Slip one stitch as if to knit, slip another stitch as if to knit. Insert left-hand needle into front of these 2 stitches and knit them together
k2tog		Knit two stitches together as one stitch
Central Double Dec		Slip first and second stitches together as if to knit. Knit 1 stitch. Pass two slipped stitches over the knit stitch.

ALTHEA CLUTCH

by illitilli

FINISHED MEASUREMENTS

9.25" wide x 1.25" deep at base; 5" high

YARN

Knit Picks Galileo (50% Merino Wool, 50% Viscose from Bamboo; 131 yards/50g): MC Gosling 26576, C1 Firefly 26101, 1 ball each.

NEEDLES

US 2 (3mm) DPNs, or 32" or longer circular needle for Magic Loop technique, or size to obtain gauge
US 6 (4mm) DPNs, or four sizes larger than size to obtain gauge

NOTIONS

Lining Fabric, approximately 12"x14"
Fusible Interfacing, Medium to Heavy Weight, approximately 12"x12"
Sewing Needle and Thread
Button, 0.75" or larger
Magnetic Snap, 1/2" diameter
Yarn Needle
Stitch Marker
Scrap Yarn or Stitch Holder
Corrugated Cardboard, 11"x14"
Packing Tape or Plastic Wrap
Iron

GAUGE

21 sts and 40 rows = 4" in Reverse St st in the round on smaller needles, blocked. Gauge is not critical for this project, but will affect the stiffness and opacity of the fabric and the size of the required lining.

Althea Clutch

Notes:

Starting with a provisional cast on, the base of the clutch is worked flat. Stitches are then picked up along the sides and joined with the live and provisionally cast on stitches to work the remainder of the bag in the round. An I-cord strap is worked separately, to be grafted to the bag body after the button and lining are in place. The lining is made from a single piece of faced fabric, folded and stitched by hand.

If you prefer not to use a provisional cast on, simply create the same number of stitches called for in the instructions using your favorite cast on method, and pick up the required number of stitches later when asked to transfer provisional stitches to the working needle.

Stockinette Stitch (St st, worked flat over any number of sts)
Row 1 (RS): Knit.
Row 2 (WS): Purl.
Rep Rows 1-2 for pattern.

DIRECTIONS
Clutch Body
Using C1 and smaller needles, provisionally CO 50 sts.
Rows 1-12: Work in St st, slipping the first st of each row and ending with a WS P row.

Pick Up Sts for Working in the Round
Step 1: With P side facing, PU and P TBL the first slipped st to the left of the live sts. (Note: This st must be twisted via the TBL as it is connected to the last live st on the needle.)
Step 2: PU and P the remaining 5 slipped sts along the left side of your knit rectangle.
Step 3: Remove waste yarn from provisional CO and transfer sts to working needle and P across.
Step 4: PU and P the 6 slipped sts from right edge of your knit rectangle. The P side of the fabric is now the RS. PM for start of rnd. 112 sts.

Rnds 1-15: Work 15 rnds in Reverse St st, purling all sts.
Rnd 16: K56, M1, K to end of rnd. Break C1 and join MC. 113 sts.
Rnd 17: K.
Rnd 18: *K1, P1; rep from * to last st, K1.
Rnd 19: *P1, K1; rep from * to last st, P1.
Rep Rnds 18 and 19 fifteen more times.

I-cord BO
Provisionally CO 4 sts onto the working needle with MC.
Using larger needle for the right needle, *K3, K2tog TBL, Sl 4 worked sts back to left needle; rep from * to last 4 sts.
Break MC, leaving a tail of 12". Graft the 4 live sts to the 4 CO sts using the Kitchener Stitch method to complete the I-cord BO.

I-cord Button Closure
Using smaller needles and MC, provisionally CO 3 sts, leaving a 12" tail of the working yarn at the start of the CO.
With DPN's, *K3, do not turn work but slide 3 sts back to right end of DPN; rep from * until I-cord measures 6".
Break yarn, leaving a tail of 12". Place the three live sts on a stitch holder or scrap yarn and set aside for finishing.

Finishing
Weave in ends on clutch body.

Blocking
Create a blocking form by cutting, scoring, folding and taping a piece of corrugated cardboard as shown in Diagram A. To prevent the cardboard form from losing its shape while blocking, wrap it completely in packing tape or plastic wrap. Wash and block the clutch on the form, propping the form upside down until the fabric is dry. Soak the I-cord button closure and block in a hanging position, stretching it gently while wet to remove some of its elasticity.

Diagram A

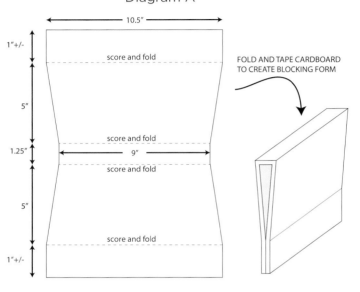

Construct Lining
Adjust the lining and facing sizes to suit your blocked knitting - you may find it useful to cut and assemble a paper template of the lining to test for fit.
Measure and cut two 1" x 10.5" pieces of fusible interfacing.
Measure and cut another 10.5" x 10.25" piece of fusible interfacing, and cut one 1.25" x 0.625" notch on each of the shorter sides of this rectangle as shown in Diagram B. Using a hot, dry iron, fuse the facings to the wrong side of your lining fabric as shown.

Cut out around the perimeter of the faced lining, leaving a 0.25" seam allowance as shown.

Diagram B

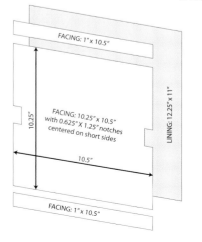

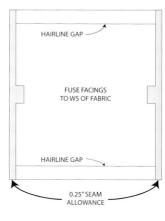

Fold the lining in half and sew the side seams using a sewing needle and thread and a running stitch. Clip the tip of the seam allowance at the corner points as shown in Diagram C and press the seams open with your fingers. Sew across the points at each end of the bottom, fold up the resulting triangular flap, and tack the flap to the side seams (see Diagram D) – this forms the squared ends of the lining bottom.

Diagram C

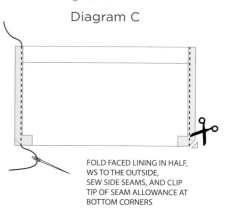

FOLD FACED LINING IN HALF,
WS TO THE OUTSIDE,
SEW SIDE SEAMS, AND CLIP
TIP OF SEAM ALLOWANCE AT
BOTTOM CORNERS

Diagram D

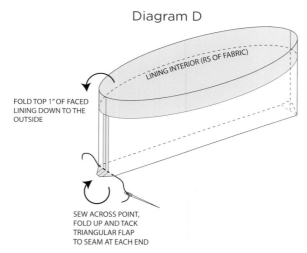

LINING INTERIOR (RS OF FABRIC)

FOLD TOP 1" OF FACED
LINING DOWN TO THE
OUTSIDE

SEW ACROSS POINT,
FOLD UP AND TACK
TRIANGULAR FLAP
TO SEAM AT EACH END

Magnetic Snap

Attach one half of the magnetic snap to each side of the lining opening at the center points, approximately 0.5" down from the top edge.

Attach Lining

Insert the lining into the knitted clutch, aligning the slipped sts at the bottom of the clutch to the bottom corner points of the lining, and the top edge of the lining to the underside of the I-cord BO. Check to make sure the lining seams do not show on the outside of the bag, and if necessary, tack and/or trim the seam allowances to achieve a smooth finish. Pin the lining in place. Using a sewing needle and thread and a whip stitch, sew the upper edge of the lining to the inside of the I-cord.

Attach Button

Measure and mark the placement of your button with a pin on the clutch front. Allow for a little space behind the button for the I-cord strap by creating a button shank: Using a sewing needle and thread, sew the button to the knitted bag and lining with

a skewer or small gauge knitting needle placed between the button and the knit fabric (see Diagram E); after sewing through the buttonholes several times, remove the skewer and wrap the sewing thread tightly around the thread loops that hold the button to reinforce the shank, then sew through the shank to the lining and secure the thread ends.

Diagram E

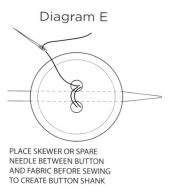

PLACE SKEWER OR SPARE
NEEDLE BETWEEN BUTTON
AND FABRIC BEFORE SEWING
TO CREATE BUTTON SHANK

Attach I-cord Strap

Use pins to mark attachment points for the I-cord strap 3" in from each side along the back of the clutch, just below the I-cord bind off. Release the three provisional CO sts from one end of the I-cord and graft to one of the marked points. Pull the cord across the front of the clutch, snugly under the button shank and up to the other pin. Stretch the cord gently – it should be taut enough to help close the clutch opening, but not so tight that it warps the top of the clutch. Unravel the I-cord to the correct length and graft the three live sts to the marked point. Weave ends into the center of the I-cord.

GUAPA MITTENS

by Kristen Jancuk

FINISHED MEASUREMENTS

7 (7.75, 8.25)" hand circumference x 8.5 (9, 9.75)" total length

YARN

Knit Picks Paragon (50% Fine Merino, 25% Baby Alpaca, 25% Mulberry Silk; 123 yards/50g): Enchanted 26973, 2 balls.

NEEDLES

US 4 (3.5mm) DPNs or two 24" circular needles for two circulars technique, or one 32" or longer circular needle for Magic Loop technique, or size to obtain gauge

US 2 (3mm) DPNs or two 24" circular needles for two circulars technique, or one 32" or longer circular needle for Magic Loop technique, or 2 sizes smaller than needle used to obtain gauge

NOTIONS

Yarn Needle
Stitch Markers
Cable Needle
Scrap Yarn or Stitch Holder

GAUGE

26 sts and 36 rounds = 4" in St st in the round on larger needles, blocked.

Guapa Mittens

Notes:

These sophisticated mittens are decorated with an expanding panel of stockinette stitch shaped with simple cables and dotted with sweet bow stitches. They're worked in the round from the cuff to the fingertips.

Bow: Insert RH needle under the 3 strands of yarn at the front of the work, from bottom to top, and then into the first st on LH needle; knit, pulling working yarn under the 3 strands of yarn before dropping LH st from needle.

DIRECTIONS
Left Mitten
Cuff
With smaller needles, CO 42 (46, 50) sts. PM and join to work in the rnd, being careful not to twist.
Rnd 1: (K1, P1) to end.
Rep Rnd 1 until cuff measures 2" or desired length.
Switch to larger needles.
Next Rnd: K5, M1L, *K 8 (9, 10), M1L; work from * a total of 4 times, K 5 to end. 47 (51, 55) sts.

Hand
Setup Rnd: K1, PM for end of thumb gusset, P 8 (9, 10), K7, P 8 (9, 10), PM, K to end.
Rnd 1: M1R, K to M, M1L, SM, work Rnd 1 of Hand Chart to next M, K to end. 2 gusset sts inc.
Rnds 2 and 3: K to M, work Hand Chart as established to next M, K to end.
Rep Rnds 1-3 a total of 7 (8, 9) times, until you have 15 (17, 19) sts between Ms for thumb gusset. 61 (67, 73) sts.
Next Rnd: Sl next 15 (17, 19) sts to stitch holder or scrap yarn, remove M, pull working yarn tightly across gap and work as established to end of rnd. 46 (50, 54) sts.

Continue mitten as established until it measures 6 (6.5, 7.25)", from top of cuff, or approximately .5" shorter than desired length, ending after Rnd 45 or 51.

Top Shaping
Rnd 1: *K 1 (3, 1), K2tog, (K2, K2tog) to M; rep from * once. 34 (38, 40) sts.
Rnd 2: Knit.
Rnd 3: *K 0 (2, 0), K2tog, (K1, K2tog) to M; rep from * once. 22 (26, 26) sts.
Rnd 4: Knit.
Rnd 5: K2tog to end. (11, 13, 13) sts.
Cut yarn, pull through remaining live sts tightly and secure to close top.
Proceed to Thumbs.

Right Mitten
Cuff
Work as for Left Mitten.

Hand
Setup Rnd: P 8 (9, 10), K7, P 8 (9, 10), PM for thumb gusset, K1, PM, K to end.

Rnd 1: Work Hand Chart to M, SM, M1R, K to M, M1L, SM, K to end.
Rnds 2 and 3: Work Hand Chart to M, K to end.
Rep Rnds 1-3 until you have 15 (17, 19) sts between Ms for thumb.
Next Rnd: Work as established to M, remove M, Sl next 15 (17, 19) sts to stitch holder or scrap yarn, remove M, pull working yarn tightly across gap and work as established to end of rnd.

Work remainder of mitten as for Left Mitten, proceed to Thumbs.

Thumbs (both hands)
Return held thumb sts to needles; divide evenly over DPNs and join yarn.

Pick up 1 st at base of thumb, K across. 16 (18, 20) sts.
PM and join to work in the rnd.
Work thumb in St st until thumb measures 1.75", or .25" shorter than desired length.

Next Rnd: K2tog to end. 8 (9, 10) sts.
Next Rnd: Knit.
Next Rnd: K 0 (1, 0), K2tog to end. 4 (5, 5) sts.

Cut yarn and pull through remaining live sts to fasten off.

Finishing
Weave in ends, using tail to close up any gaps at base of thumb. Wash and block gently.

Hand Chart

Legend

Symbol	Name	Description
•	**purl**	purl stitch
⊻⊠	**c2 over 1 right**	sl1 to CN, hold in back. k2, k1 from CN
☐	**knit**	knit stitch
⊠⊼	**c2 over 1 left**	sl2 to CN, hold in front. k1, k2 from CN
V	**slip wyif**	Slip stitch as if to purl, with yarn in front
⌘	**Bow**	Insert RH needle under the 3 strands of yarn at the front of the work, from bottom to top, and then into the first st on LH needle; knit, pulling working yarn under the 3 strands of yarn before dropping LH st from needle
☐	**pattern repeat**	

Notes:
For size 7", begin at st 3 and end at st 25.
For size 7.75", begin at st 2 and end at st 26
For size 8.25", begin at st 1 and end at st 27.

Chart rows are read from right to left across each round.

PIMA COWL

by Tamara Moots

FINISHED MEASUREMENTS
26" circumference x 9" tall

YARN
Knit Picks Gloss DK (70% Merino Wool, 30% Silk; 123 yards/50g): Topaz 27011, 2 balls.

NEEDLES
US 6 (4mm) 16" circular needle, or size to obtain gauge

NOTIONS
Yarn Needle
Stitch Marker
Cable Needle

GAUGE
22 sts and 26 rows = 4" in Living Tapestry Pattern in the rnd, blocked.

Pima Cowl

Notes:

The Pima Cowl combines luxury yarn with simple cables to evoke the living tapestry and beauty of the Sonoran Desert. Named after one of my favorite places on the on the planet and also one of the Desert Peoples of the area famous for their basket and textiles. Cables are written and charted.

See Chart Key for instructions to work Cables within pattern.
Read each chart row from right to left, repeating the row 9 times across the round.

Garter St (worked in the rnd over any number of sts)
Rnd 1: K.
Rnd 2: P.
Rep Rnds 1-2 for pattern.

DIRECTIONS

CO 144 sts. PM. Join in the rnd being careful not to twist.

Beginning Edging

Work 9 rnds in Garter St.

Using either written directions or chart, work Living Tapestry Pattern Rnds 1-20 two times.
Work Rnd 1 one additional time.

Living Tapestry Pattern

20 rnds, multiples of 16 sts repeated around.
Rnd 1: *P4, K8, P4; rep from * to end.
Rnd 2: *P4, 2/2 RC, 2/2 LC, P4; rep from * to end.

Rnd 3: *P4, K8, P4; rep from * to end.
Rnd 4: *P3, 2/1 RPC, K4, 2/1 LPC, P3; rep from * to end.
Rnd 5: *P3, K2, P1, K4, P1, K2, P3; rep from * to end.
Rnd 6: *P2, 2/1 RPC, P1, K4, P1, 2/1 LPC, P2; rep from * to end.
Rnd 7: *P2, K2, P2, K4, P2, K2, P2; rep from * to end.
Rnd 8: *P1, 2/1 RPC, P2, K4, P2, 2/1 LPC, P1; rep from * to end.
Rnd 9: *P1, K2, P10, K2, P1; rep from * to end.
Rnd 10: *2/1 RPC, P3, K4, P3, 2/1 LPC; rep from * to end.
Rnd 11: *K2, P12, K2; rep from * to 2 sts before end of rnd, working last rep as K2, P12. Note: The last K2 of Rnd 11 will be left unworked and used instead for the first 2/2 LC on Rnd 12.
Rnd 12: Using the last 2 sts of Rnd 11, slip 2 sts to CN and hold in front, remove marker, K2 from LH needle, replace marker, K2 from CN, P4, K4, P4, 2/2 LC, *2/2 LC, P4, K4, P4, 2/2 LC; rep from * to last 2 sts, K2.
Rnd 13: *K2, P12, K2; rep from * to end.
Rnd 14: *2/1 LPC, P3, K4, P3, 2/1 RPC; rep from * to end.
Rnd 15: *P1, K2, P3, K4, P3, K2, P1; rep from * to end.
Rnd 16: *P1, 2/1 LPC, P2, K4, P2, 2/1 RPC, P1; rep from * to end.
Rnd 17: *P2, K2, P2, K4, P2, K2, P2; rep from * to end.
Rnd 18: *P2, 2/1 LPC, P1, K4, P1, 2/1 RPC, P2; rep from * to end.
Rnd 19: *P3, K2, P1, K4, P1, K2, P3; rep from * to end.
Rnd 20: *P3, 2/1 LPC, K4, 2/1 RPC, P3; rep from * to end.

Ending Edging

Work 9 rnds in Garter St.

Finishing

Bind off. Weave in ends. Wash and block as desired.

Living Tapestry Chart

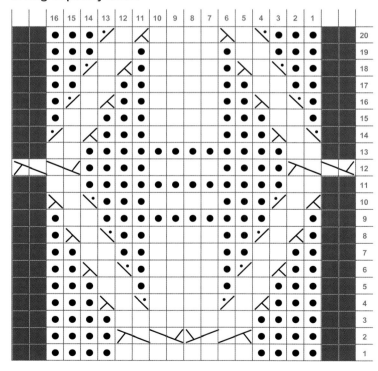

Legend

No Stitch
Placeholder - No stitch made.

2/2 LC
sl 2 to CN, hold in front.
k2, k2 from CN

2/1 RPC
sl1 to CN, hold in back.
k2, p1 from CN

2/1 LPC
sl2 to CN, hold in front.
p1, k2 from CN

purl
purl stitch

knit
knit stitch

ALPINE SHAWL

by Tetiana Otruta

FINISHED MEASUREMENTS

65" wingspan, 25" deep, relaxed after blocking.

YARN

Knit Picks Luminance (100% Silk; 439 yards/50g): Brilliance 27052, 2 hanks.

NEEDLES

US 6 (4 mm) 32" or longer circular needle, or size to obtain gauge.

NOTIONS

Stitch Markers, one of a different color
Yarn Needle

GAUGE

18 sts and 25 rows = 4" in St st with yarn held double, blocked.

Alpine Shawl

Notes:

This elegant shaw is a half circle, worked from center back to bottom edge. It's knitted with the yarn held double.

Read Chart A and B from right to left. Wrong side rows are not shown on the charts, work them as K2, P to 2 sts from end, K2.

BO P-wise: P1, *P1, pull the first st on the RH needle over the second st and off the right needle, repeat from * to end.

M1P: Lift loop between sts with LH needle, P1 TBL.

YO2: YO, twice.

DIRECTIONS
Setup Rows
CO 3 sts with yarn held double.
Row 1 (RS): K1, KFB, K1. 4 sts.
Row 2 (WS): K1, M1, K2, M1, K1. 6 sts.
Row 3: K2, YO, K1, YO, K1, YO, K2. 9 sts.
Row 4: K2, P5, K2.

Part 1, Chart A
Row 1 (RS): K2, YO, K2, PM, YO, K1, YO, PM, K2, YO, K2. 13 sts.
Row 2 and WS Rows through Row 16: K2, P to 2 sts from end, K2.
Row 3: K2, YO, K3, SM, YO, K3, YO, SM, K3, YO, K2. 17 sts.
Row 5: K2, YO, K4, SM, YO, K2, YO, K2TOG, K1, YO, SM, K4, YO, K2. 21 sts.
Row 7: K2, YO, K5, SM, YO, K7, YO, SM, K5, YO, K2. 25 sts.
Row 9: K2, YO, K6, SM, YO, K2, YO, SKP, K1, K2TOG, YO, K2, YO, SM, K6, YO, K2. 29 sts.
Row 11: K2, YO, K7, SM, YO, K4, YO, SK2P, YO, K4, YO, SM, K7, YO, K2. 33 sts.
Row 13: K2, YO, K8, SM, YO, K2, YO, SKP, K5, K2TOG, YO, K2, YO, SM, K8, YO, K2. 37 sts.
Row 15: K2, YO, K9, SM, YO, K4, YO, SKP, K1, PM of different color, YO, PM, SKP, K2TOG, YO, K4, YO, SM, K9, YO, K2. 41 sts.

Part 2, Chart B
Work Chart B Rows 1-16 seven times total, repeating the group of sts in brackets (outlined in red pattern repeat on the Chart) as many times as the repeat number you are working.
For example: For the 3rd repeat of Rows 1-16, work sts in brackets, or outlined in red on the chart, 3 times, then continue row as directed.
4 sts inc each RS row, 1 in the St st section on either side of the lace panel, and 2 in the lace panel.

Row 1 (RS): K2, YO, K to M, [SM, YO, K2, YO, SKP, K2, K2TOG] rep*, SM, YO, K1, YO, SM, [SKP, K2, K2TOG, YO, K2, YO, SM] rep*, K to 2 sts from end, YO, K2.
Row 2 and WS Rows through Row 16: K2, P to 2 sts from end, K2.
Row 3: K2, YO, K to M, [SM, YO, K4, YO, SKP, K2TOG] rep*, SM, YO, K3, YO, SM, [SKP, K2TOG, YO, K4, YO, SM] rep* times, K to 2 sts from end, YO, K2.
Row 5: K2, YO, K to M, [SM, YO, K2, YO, SKP, K2, K2TOG] rep*, SM, YO, K2, YO, K2TOG, K1, YO, SM, [SKP, K2, K2TOG, YO, K2, YO, SM] rep*, K to 2 sts from end, YO, K2.

Row 7: K2, YO, K to M, [SM, YO, K4, YO, SKP, K2TOG] rep*, SM, YO, K7, YO, SM, [SKP, K2TOG, YO, K4, YO, SM] rep*, K to 2 sts from end, YO, K2.
Row 9: K2, YO, K to M, [SM, YO, K2, YO, SKP, K2, K2TOG] rep*, SM, YO, K2, YO, SKP, K1, K2TOG, YO, K2, YO, SM, [SKP, K2, K2TOG, YO, K2, YO, SM] rep*, K to 2 sts from end, YO, K2.
Row 11: K2, YO, K to M, [SM, YO, K4, YO, SKP, K2TOG] rep*, SM, YO, K4, YO, SK2P, YO, K4, YO, SM, [SKP, K2TOG, YO, K4, YO, SM] rep*, K to 2 sts from end, YO, K2.
Row 13: K2, YO, K to M, [SM, YO, K2, YO, SKP, K2, K2TOG] rep*, SM, YO, K2, YO, SKP, K5, K2TOG, YO, K2, YO, SM, [SKP, K2, K2TOG, YO, K2, YO, SM] rep*, K to 2 sts from end, YO, K2.
Row 15: K2, YO, K to M, [SM, YO, K4, YO, SKP, K2TOG] rep*, SM, YO, K4, YO, SKP, K1, PM, YO, PM, SKP, K2TOG, YO, K4, YO, SM, [SKP, K2TOG, YO, K4, YO, SM] rep*, K to 2 sts from end, YO, K2.

After the 7th rep of Rows 1-16, there are 265 sts. Work Rows 1-2 once, rep sts in brackets 8 times, slipping newly placed markers. 269 sts.

Next Row (RS): K2, YO, K to M, SM, *YO, K4, YO, SKP, K2TOG, remove M; rep from * a total of 8 times, YO, K1, SM, K1, SM, K1, YO, *remove M, SKP, K2TOG, YO, K4, YO; rep from * a total of 8 times, SM, K to 2 sts from end, YO, K2. 273 sts.
Next Row (WS): K2, P to 2 sts from end, K2.

Part 3, Edge
Row 1 (RS): K2, YO, P to M, SM, M1P, P to M, SM, P1, SM, P to M, M1P, SM, P to 2 sts from end, YO, K2. 277 sts.
Rows 2, 4, 6, 8, 10 (WS): K2, P to 2 sts from end, K2.
Row 3: Rep Row 1. 281 sts.
Row 5: K2, YO, (K2TOG, YO) rep to M, SM, (K2TOG, YO) rep to M, SM, K1, SM, (YO, SKP) rep to M, SM, (YO, SKP) rep to 2 sts from end, YO, K2. 283 sts.
Row 7: Rep Row 1. 287 sts.
Row 9: Rep Row 1, removing all markers. 291 sts.
Row 11: P7, *P2TOG, YO2, P2TOG, P4; rep from * to 4 sts from end, P4. 291 sts.
Row 12: P9, *(P1, K1) 3 times into YO2 loops, P6; rep from * to 2 sts from end, P2. 431 sts.

Bind Off
Using a Cable CO is recommended. CO sts onto the LH needle.

Bind Off Row (RS): CO 2 sts, BO 12 sts P-wise, *move last st to LH needle from RH needle, CO 2 sts, BO 14 sts P-wise; rep from * to 12 sts from end. Move last st to LH needle from RH needle, CO 2 sts, BO 13 sts P-wise, move last st to LH needle from RH needle, CO 2 sts, BO 3 sts P-wise.

Break yarn, draw tail through last st to fasten off.

Finishing
Weave in yarn ends; trim after blocking. Soak shawl in lukewarm water (with soap for fiber if desired) for 10-15 minutes. Rinse and roll in towel to get rid of excess water. Pin out on a clean sheet or blocking board. Let dry and unpin only when dry, then trim yarn tails.

Chart A

| 41 | 40 | 39 | 38 | 37 | 36 | 35 | 34 | 33 | 32 | 31 | 30 | 29 | 28 | 27 | 26 | 25 | 24 | 23 | 22 | 21 | 20 | 19 | 18 | 17 | 16 | 15 | 14 | 13 | 12 | 11 | 10 | 9 | 8 | 7 | 6 | 5 | 4 | 3 | 2 | 1 | |

Chart B

*Work the increased stitch in St st

St st*

Legend

☐ **knit**
Knit stitch

⊙ **yo**
Yarn over

▦ **No Stitch**
Placeholder - No stitch made

λ **skp**
slip 1, knit 1, pass slipped stitch over knit 1

Λ **sk2p**
Slip first stitch as if to knit. Knit 2 tog, Pass slipped stitch over the k2tog

— **PM**

— **pattern repeat**

╱ **k2tog**
Knit two stitches together as one stitch

DECLINATION COWL

by Triona Murphy

FINISHED MEASUREMENTS
26" circumference x 6.75" tall

YARN
Knit Picks Capra DK (85% Merino Wool, 15% Cashmere; 123 yards/50g): Urchin 26556, 2 balls.

NEEDLES
US 5 (3.75mm) 24" circular needles or 1 size smaller than size to obtain gauge
US 6 (4mm) 24" circular needles or size to obtain gauge

NOTIONS
Stitch Marker
Yarn Needle

GAUGE
24 sts and 32 rows = 4" in Slipped Diagonals Pattern on larger needles, blocked

Declination Cowl

Notes:

This cowl is worked in the round from the bottom edge to the top.

If you'd prefer a taller or shorter cowl, it's easy to adjust the size by working a few more or fewer repeats of the Slipped Diagonals pattern before the last section of ribbing.

Read each chart row from right to left, repeating the chart 26 times across the round.

2x2 Rib (worked in the rnd over a multiple of 4 sts)
Rnd 1: (K2, P2) to end.
Rep Rnd 1 for pattern.

Slipped Diagonals Pattern (worked in the rnd over a multiple of 6 sts)
Rnd 1: (Sl 3 P-wise WYIF, K3) to end.
Rnd 2: (K1, Sl 3 P-wise WYIF, K2) to end.
Rnd 3: (K2, Sl 3 P-wise WYIF, K1) to end.
Rnd 4: (K3, Sl 3 P-wise WYIF) to end.
Rnds 5 and 6: Knit all sts.
Rep Rnds 1-6 for pattern.

DIRECTIONS

With smaller circular needles, CO 156 sts. PM and join for working in the rnd, being careful not to twist.

Work 2x2 Rib for 1". Switch to larger circular needles and knit two rnds.

Begin Slipped Diagonals Pattern, working from chart or written instructions.
Work 6 repeats of pattern in total (piece should measure approximately 5.75" from CO edge).

Switch to smaller circular needles and work 2x2 Rib for 1". BO all sts loosely in pattern.

Finishing
Weave in ends and block.

Slipped Diagonals Chart

6	5	4	3	2	1	
						6
						5
V	V	V				4
	V	V	V			3
		V	V	V		2
			V	V	V	1

Legend

slip wyif
☑ Slip stitch as if to purl, with yarn in front

knit
☐ knit stitch

ADELAIDA HAT

by Irina Anikeeva

FINISHED MEASUREMENTS

17.75" brim circumference x 8.5" high, to fit head sizes 20-23".

YARN

Knit Picks Capretta (80% Fine Merino Wool, 10% Cashmere, 10% Nylon; 230 yards/50g): Celestial 25597, 1 ball

NEEDLES

US 3 (3.25mm) 16" circular needles plus DPNs, or size to obtain gauge
US 1 (2.25mm) 16" circular needles, or 2 sizes smaller than those to obtain gauge

NOTIONS

Stitch Markers
Yarn Needle

GAUGE

27 sts and 40 rnds = 4" over Body Chart in the rnd on larger needles, blocked.

Adelaida Hat

Notes:

Hat is worked from brim to crown in the round. All rounds on the chart are read from right to left. Knitters may consider placing markers between the chart repeats.

Body Chart (worked in rnd over multiple of 24 sts, rep 5x per rnd)

Rnd 1: K3, SSK, K5, YO, SSK, YO, K1, YO, K2tog, YO, K5, K2tog, K2.

Rnd 2 and all even rnds through Rnd 24: K.

Rnd 3: K3, SSK, K4, YO, SSK, YO, K3, YO, K2tog, YO, K4, K2tog, K2.

Rnd 5: K3, SSK, K3, (YO, SSK) 2x, YO, K1, (YO, K2tog) 2x, YO, K3, K2tog, K2.

Rnd 7: K3, SSK, K2, (YO, SSK) 2x, YO, K3, (YO, K2tog) 2x, YO, K2, K2tog, K2.

Rnd 9: K3, SSK, K1, (YO, SSK) 2x, YO, K5, (YO, K2tog) 2x, YO, K1, K2tog, K2.

Rnd 11: K3, (SSK, YO) 3x, K7, (YO, K2tog) 3x, K2.

Rnd 13: K1, YO, K2tog, YO, K5, K2tog, K5, SSK, K5, YO, SSK, YO.

Rnd 15: K2, YO, K2tog, YO, K4, K2tog, K5, SSK, K4, YO, SSK, YO, K1.

Rnd 17: K1, (YO, K2tog) 2x, YO, K3, K2tog, K5, SSK, K3, (YO, SSK) 2x, YO.

Rnd 19: K2, (YO, K2tog) 2x, YO, K2, K2tog, K5, SSK, K2, (YO, SSK) 2x, YO, K1.

Rnd 21: K3, (YO, K2tog) 2x, YO, K1, K2tog, K5, SSK, K1, (YO, SSK) 2x, YO, K2.

Rnd 23: K4, (YO, K2tog) 3x, K5, (SSK, YO) 3x, K3.

Crown Chart (worked in the rnd over a multiple of 24 sts, rep 5x per rnd)

Rnds 1-12: Rep Body Chart Rnds 1-12.

Rnd 13: K1, K2tog, YO, K5, K2tog, K5, SSK, K5, YO, SSK. 110 sts.

Rnd 14 and all even rnds through Rnd 22: K.

Rnd 15: K1, K2tog, YO, K4, K2tog, K5, SSK, K4, YO, SSK. 100 sts.

Rnd 17: K1, K2tog, YO, K3, K2tog, K5, SSK, K3, YO, SSK. 90 sts.

Rnd 19: K1, K2tog, YO, K2, K2tog, K5, SSK, K2, YO, SSK. 80 sts.

Rnd 21: K1, K2tog, YO, K1, K2tog, K5, SSK, K1, YO, SSK. 70 sts.

Rnd 23: K1, K2tog, YO, K2tog, K1, CDD, K1, SSK, YO, SSK. 50 sts.

Rnd 24: K4, CDD, K3. 40 sts.

Rnd 25: K3, CDD, K2. 30 sts.

Rnd 26: K2, CDD, K1. 20 sts.

Rnd 27: K1, CDD. 10 sts.

DIRECTIONS

Brim

With smaller circular needle loosely CO 120 sts. PM and join in rnd, being careful not to twist sts.

Ribbing Round: *K1 TBL, P1; rep from * to the end of rnd.

Rep the Ribbing Round 11 more times.

Body

Switch to larger circular needle as you work the next rnd.

Work 24-st rep of Body Chart five times around, working Rnds 1-24 twice.

Crown

Work Rnds 1-27 of Crown Chart, changing to DPNs when sts no longer feel comfortable on circular needle. 10 sts.

Cut yarn, leaving an 8" tail. Using yarn needle, thread yarn tail through remaining sts two times, then pull tightly.

Finishing

Weave in yarn ends. Block to measurements.

Legend

knit
knit stitch

ssk
Slip one stitch as if to knit, slip another stitch as if to knit. Insert left-hand needle into front of these 2 stitches and knit them together

yo
yarn over

k2tog
Knit two stitches together as one stitch

Central Double Dec
Slip first and second stitches together as if to knit. Knit 1 stitch. Pass two slipped stitches over the knit stitch.

No Stitch
Placeholder - No stitch made

Body Chart

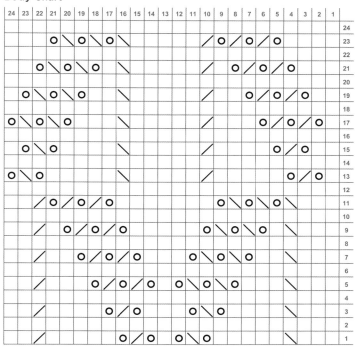

Crown Chart

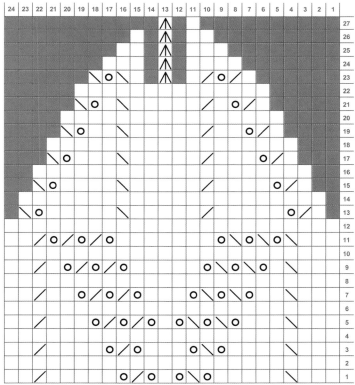

BLITHE COWL

by Martha Wissing

FINISHED MEASUREMENTS
12.25x36 (60)"

YARN
Knit Picks Aloft (72% Super Kid Mohair, 28% Silk; 260 yards/25g): Eggplant 25210, 2 (3) balls

NEEDLES
US 6 (4mm) straight or circular needles, or size to obtain gauge

NOTIONS
Yarn Needle

Stitch Markers
Scrap Yarn for Provisional CO
Spare US 6 (4mm) or smaller needle for 3-Needle BO

GAUGE
20 sts and 26 rows = 4" in Lace pattern, blocked.
20 sts and 36 rows = 4" in Brioche pattern, blocked.

Blithe Cowl

Notes:

This cowl begins with a provisional cast on, followed by sections of garter, brioche, garter and lace repeated for the length of the cowl. A 3-Needle Bind Off joins the cowl. Slip sts as if to purl.

YF-Sl1-YO: Yarn forward, SL 1, yarn over needle.

Brioche Knit (BRK): Knit the st and its YO together.

DIRECTIONS

Using scrap yarn, provisionally CO 61 sts. With working yarn, knit 1 row.

First Garter Section

Row 1 (RS): Sl2 WYIB, P1, K to last 3 sts, P1, K2.

Row 2 (WS): Sl2 WYIF, K to last 2 sts, P2.

Rep Rows 1 & 2 once.

Brioche Section

Brioche Set-up Row (RS): Sl2 WYIB, P1, *YF-Sl1-YO, K1; rep from * to last 4 sts, YF-Sl1-YO, P1, K2.

Row 1 (WS): Sl2 WYIF, K1, *BRK, YF-Sl1-YO; rep from * to last 4 sts, BRK, K1, P2.

Row 2 (RS): Sl2 WYIB, P1, * YF-Sl1-YO, BRK; rep from * to last 4 sts, YF-Sl1-YO, P1, K2.

Rep Rows 1 & 2 until piece measures 6", ending with a RS row.

Next Row (WS): Sl2 WYIF, K1, *BRK, K1; rep from * to last 4 sts, BRK, K1, P2.

Second Garter Section

Row 1 (RS): Sl2 WYIB, P1, K to last 3 sts, P1, K2.

Row 2 (WS): Sl2 WYIF, K to last 2 sts, P2.

Rep Rows 1 & 2 three times.

Lace Section

Rows 1, 3 and 5 (RS): Sl2 WYIB, P1, K1, *YO, SSK, K1, K2tog, YO, K1; rep from * to last 3 sts, P1, K2.

Row 2 and all WS rows: Sl2 WYIF, K1, P to last 3 sts, K1, P2.

Row 7: Sl2 WYIB, P1, K2, *YO, Sk2p, YO, K3; rep from * to last 8 sts, YO, Sk2p, YO, K2, P1, K2.

Row 9: Sl2 WYIB, P1, K1, *K2tog, YO, K1, YO, SSK, K1; rep from * to last 3 sts, P1, K2.

Row 11: Sl2 WYIB, P1, K2tog, *YO, K3, YO, Sk2p; rep from * to last 8 sts, YO, K3, YO, SSK, P1, K2.

Row 12: Sl2 WYIF, K1, P to last 3 sts, K1, P2.

Rep Rows 1 – 12 once more.

Rep Rows 1 – 8.

Piece should measure approximately 12".

Rep First Garter, Brioche, Second Garter, and Lace Sections 2 (4) times more. Piece should measure 36 (60)".

Finishing

Steam block to Finished Measurements before seaming.

Join into Cowl: Remove Provisional CO, putting the 61 sts on spare needle. With right sides together being careful not to twist, work 3-Needle BO. Weave in ends.

MEANDERING LACE SHAWLETTE

by Mone Dräger

FINISHED MEASUREMENTS
14" deep x 60" across top edge

YARN
Knit Picks Diadem Fingering (50% Alpaca, 50% Silk; 329 yards/100g): Gold 26530, 1 hank

NEEDLES
US 5 (3.75mm) straight or 16" or longer circular needles, or size to obtain gauge

NOTIONS
Yarn Needle
Stitch Marker

GAUGE
14 sts and 28 rows = 4" in Garter stitch, blocked. (Gauge is not crucial for this project, but will affect the finished size and yardage needed.)

Meandering Lace Shawlette

Notes:

This shawlette is knit sideways, featuring a beautiful meandering lace border. The construction method makes best use of one skein of yarn, as the shawlette is knit from one narrow point to the other. Increases turn into decreases when half of the yarn is knit up. The main part of the shawlette is knit in garter stitch. If working from the charts read RS rows from right to left, and WS rows from left to right. For the Set-Up Chart RS rows are even numbers, Main Chart and End Chart RS rows are odd numbers.

Garter Stitch (worked flat)
All Rows: Knit.

Meandering Lace Set-Up Chart (worked flat)
Row 1 (WS): YO, P2. 3 sts.
Row 2 (RS): K1, YO, SSK.
Row 3: YO, P3. 4 sts.
Row 4: K2, YO, SSK.
Row 5: YO, P4. 5 sts.
Row 6: K1, (YO, SSK) twice.
Row 7: YO, P5. 6 sts.
Row 8: K2, (YO, SSK) twice.
Row 9: YO, P6. 7 sts.
Row 10: K1, (YO, SSK) three times.
Row 11: YO, P6, K1. 8 sts.
Row 12: K2, (YO SSK) three times.
Row 13: YO, P6, K2. 9 sts.
Row 14: K3, (YO, SSK) three times.
Row 15: YO, P6, K3. 10 sts.
Row 16: K4, (YO, SSK) three times.
Row 17: YO, P6, K4. 11 sts.
Row 18: K5, (YO, SSK) three times.
Row 19: YO, P6, K5. 12 sts.
Row 20: K6, (YO, SSK) three times.
Row 21: YO, P7, K5. 13 sts.
Row 22: K7, (YO, SSK) three times.
Row 23: YO, P7, K6. 14 sts.

Meandering Lace Main Chart (worked flat)
Row 1 (RS): K4, K2tog, YO, K1, (YO, SSK) three times. 13 sts.
Row 2 (WS): YO, P9, K4. 14 sts.
Row 3: K3, (K2tog, YO) twice, K1, (YO SSK) three times.
Row 4: YO, P11, K3. 15 sts.
Row 5: K2, (K2tog, YO) three times, K1, (YO, SSK) three times.
Row 6: YO, P13, K2. 16 sts.
Row 7: K1, (K2tog, YO) three times, K3, (YO, SSK) three times.
Row 8: P15, K1.
Row 9: K1, (SSK, YO) three times, K3, (YO, K2tog) three times.
Rows 10 - 16: Rep Rows 8 – 9 three times, then rep Row 8 once more.
Row 17: KFB, (SSK, YO) three times, Sk2p, (YO, K2tog) three times. 15 sts.
Row 18: P13, K2.
Row 19: K1, KFB, (SSK, YO) twice, Sk2p, (YO, K2tog) three times. 14 sts.
Row 20: P11, K3.

Row 21: K2, KFB, (SSK, YO) twice, Sk2p, (YO, K2tog) twice. 13 sts.
Row 22: P9, K4.
Row 23: K3, KFB, (SSK, YO) twice, Sk2p, YO, K2tog. 12 sts.
Row 24: P7, K5.
Row 25: K4, KFB, (YO, SSK) twice, YO, Sk2p.
Row 26: YO, P7, K5. 13 sts.
Rep Rows 1-26 for pattern.

Meandering Lace End Chart (worked flat)
Row 1 (RS): K5, (SSK, YO) three times, K3tog, (YO, K2tog) twice. 16 sts.
Row 2 (WS): P11, K5.
Row 3: K4, KFB, (SSK, YO) twice, K3tog, (YO, K2tog) twice. 15 sts.
Row 4: P10, K5.
Row 5: K5, KFB, SSK, YO, K3tog, (YO, K2tog) twice. 14 sts.
Row 6: P8, K6.
Row 7: K7, YO, K3tog, (YO, K2tog) twice. 13 sts.
Row 8: P7, K6.
Row 9: K5, (K2tog, YO) three times, K2tog. 12 sts.
Row 10: P7, K5.
Row 11: K4, (K2tog, YO) three times, K2tog. 11 sts.
Row 12: P7, K4.
Row 13: K3, (K2tog, YO) three times, K2tog. 10 sts.
Row 14: P7, K3.
Row 15: K2, (K2tog, YO) three times, K2tog. 9 sts.
Row 16: P7, K2.
Row 17: K1, (K2tog, YO) three times, K2tog. 8 sts.
Row 18: P7, K1.
Row 19: (K2tog, YO) three times, K2tog. 7 sts.
Row 20 and all even numbered rows through Row 28: Purl.
Row 21: K1, (K2tog, YO) twice, K2tog. 6 sts.
Row 23: (K2tog, YO) twice, K2tog. 5 sts.
Row 25: K1, K2tog, YO, K2tog. 4 sts.
Row 27: K2tog, YO, K2tog. 3 sts.
Row 29: K1, K2tog. 2 sts.

DIRECTIONS

Set-up Section
CO 2 sts. Work Rows 1-23 of the Meandering Lace Set-up Chart. 14 sts.

Increase Section
Row 1 (RS): K1, PM, work Row 1 of Meandering Lace Main Chart.
Row 2 and all even numbered rows through Row 8 (WS): Work to M from next row of Meandering Lace Main Chart, SM, K to end.
Row 3: KFB, SM, work to end from Meandering Lace Main Chart. 15 sts.
Row 5: K to M, SM, work to end from Meandering Lace Main Chart.
Row 7: K to 1 st before M, KFB, SM, work to end from Meandering Lace Main Chart. 1 st inc.
Rep Rows 5-8, increasing 1 st every fourth row as established 37 more times, i.e. work Rows 1 – 26 of the Meandering Lace Main Chart a total of 6 times. 53 sts; 40 sts before the marker in the Garter st section, 13 sts in the charted Lace section.

Straight Section
Row 1 (RS): K to M, SM, work to end from Meandering Lace Main Chart.

Row 2 (WS): Work to M from Meandering Lace Main Chart, SM, K to end.

Rep Rows 1-2 a total of 52 times, i.e. work Rows 1-26 of the Meandering Lace Main Chart 4 times.

Decrease Section

Row 1 (RS): K to 2 sts before M, K2tog, SM, work to end from Meandering Lace Main Chart. 1 st dec.

Rows 2 and 4 (WS): Work to M from Meandering Lace Main Chart, SM, K to end.

Row 3: K to M, SM, work to end from Meandering Lace Main Chart.

Rep Rows 1-4, decreasing 1 st every fourth row as established 36 more times, i.e. work Rows 1 – 26 of the Meandering Lace Main Chart 5 times, then work Rows 1-18 again. Remove marker on last row. 18 sts.

Final Decrease Section

Work Rows 1-29 from Meandering Lace End Chart. 2 sts. Bind off.

Finishing

Weave in ends, wash and block to Finished Measurements.

Main Chart

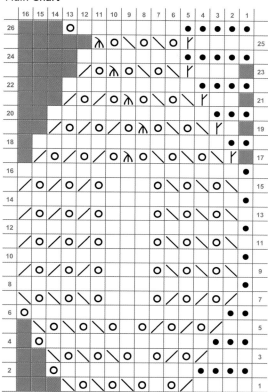

Set-up Chart

Legend

knit
RS: knit stitch
WS: purl stitch

k2tog
RS: Knit two stitches together as one stitch
WS: Purl 2 stitches together

yo
Yarn over

ssk
RS: Slip one stitch as if to knit, Slip another stitch as if to knit. Insert left-hand needle into front of these 2 stitches and knit them together
WS: Purl two stitches together in back loops, inserting needle from the left, behind and into the backs of the 2nd & 1st stitches in that order

No Stitch
Placeholder - No stitch made.

purl
RS: purl stitch
WS: knit stitch

kfb
RS: Knit into the front and back of the stitch
WS: Purl into the front and the back of the stitch

sl1 k2tog psso
slip 1, k2tog, pass slip stitch over k2tog

k3tog
RS: Knit three stitches together as one
WS: Purl three stitches together as one

End Chart

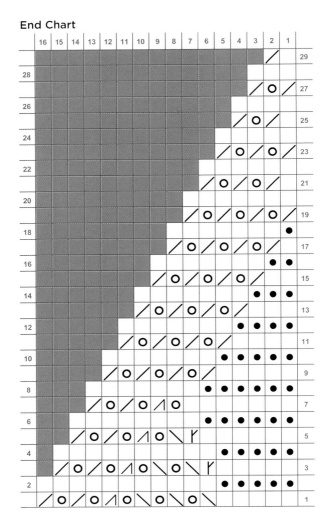

RONA COWL

by Bridget Pupillo

FINISHED MEASUREMENTS

6.5" high x 26 (28, 30)" circumference, to fit 13 (16, 19)" neck circumference

YARN

Knit Picks Capra DK (85% Merino Wool, 15% Cashmere; 123 yards/50g): Fuchsia 26560, 2 balls

NEEDLES

US 6 (4mm) straight or 16-24" circular needles, or size to obtain gauge

NOTIONS

Yarn Needle
Stitch Markers
Cable Needle
Optional: Three 0.5" decorative buttons

GAUGE

22 sts and 32 rows = 4" in Reverse Rice Stitch, blocked.
24 sts = 4.5" wide over Center Cable pattern, blocked

Rona Cowl

Notes:

The Rona Cowl is worked flat with Reverse Rice Stitch at the edges and a Knotwork Cable pattern in the center panel. The cowl is overlapped and sewn together at the bottom edges, and the optional three decorative buttons can be placed to keep the crossover in place. The cowl can be slipped easily over the head.

DIRECTIONS

Top Edging

CO 36 sts. Work 2-st rep of Reverse Rice Stitch Chart across first row.

Rep Rows 1-4 of Reverse Rice Stitch Chart for 1.5," ending on a RS row.

Next Row (WS): Continuing in Reverse Rice Stitch, work 6 sts, PM, work 24 sts, PM, work last 6 sts of row in pattern.

Cabled Section

Work to first marker in Reverse Rice Stitch, SM, work Row 1 of Center Cable Chart, SM, work to end of row in Reverse Rice Stitch.

Continue in this manner, repeating Rows 1-16 of Center Cable Chart until cowl measures 22 (24, 26)" in length.

Bottom Edging

Work across row in Reverse Rice Stitch, removing markers. Continue in Reverse Rice Stitch until cowl measures 26 (28, 30)" in length.

BO all sts. Break yarn, leaving a 36" tail for sewing.

Finishing

Wash and block to finished measurements.

Overlap the top edging of the cowl perpendicularly over bottom edging as shown in diagram. Pin in place and sew along outer side and bottom edges, using long BO tail and yarn needle. Weave in all ends.

Optional: Sew three buttons evenly spaced along inner side edge to hold bottom and top of cowl together.

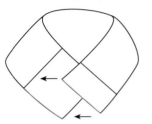

Finishing diagram

Sew sections shown in red together

Center Cable Chart

Read RS (odd numbered) rows from right to left and WS (even numbered) rows from left to right. Work across all sts of chart.

Legend

⊡	**purl** RS: purl stitch WS: knit stitch
☐	**knit** RS: knit stitch WS: purl stitch
	c2 over 2 left P sl 2 to CN, hold in front. p2, k2 from CN
	c2 over 2 right P sl2 to CN, hold in back. k2, p2 from CN
	c2 over 2 left sl 2 to CN, hold in front. k2, k2 from CN
	c2 over 2 right sl2 to CN, hold in back. k2, k2 from CN
∼	**purl tbl** WS: Knit stitch through the back loop

Reverse Rice St Chart

	2	1
4	∼	
		3
2		∼
		1

Read RS (odd numbered) rows from right to left and WS (even numbered) rows from left to right. Work 2-stitch chart repeat as noted in pattern instructions.

MONETTE HAT

by Megan Nodecker

FINISHED MEASUREMENTS
20.25 (22.25)" circumference,
10.75(11.25)" tall

YARN
Knit Picks Aloft (72% Super Kid Mohair,
28% Silk; 260 yards/25g): Carbon 25758,
2 balls

NEEDLES
US 7 (4.5mm) 16" circular needles plus
DPN's or long circular for Magic Loop
method, or size to obtain gauge

NOTIONS
Yarn Needle
Stitch Marker

GAUGE
16.5 sts and 24 rows = 4" in 2x2 Ribbing
pattern using 2 strands held together,
blocked, unstretched

Monette Hat

Notes:

This is a super stretchy, slouchy hat worked from the brim up. It is knit with two strands of Aloft held together to make a fuzzier and more substantial fabric. When you measure your swatch keep it unstretched for accuracy. Finished measurements are also taken unstretched.

2x2 Ribbing (worked in the round over a multiple of 4 sts)
All Rnds: *K2, P2, rep from * to end of rnd.

DIRECTIONS

Body

The body is worked straight from the brim to the crown.
With two strands held together, using circular needles CO 84 (92) sts, PM and join in the rnd being careful not to twist sts.
Work in 2x2 Ribbing for 9 (9.5)".

Crown

Switch to DPNs or Magic Loop when necessary.
Rnd 1: *K2, P2tog, rep from * to end of rnd. 63 (69) sts.
Rnds 2, 3, 4 and 5: *K2, P1, rep from * to end.
Rnd 6: *K2tog, P1, rep from * to end of rnd. 42 (46) sts.
Rnds 7, 8 and 9: *K1, P1, rep from * to end.
Rnd 10: remove M, K1, replace M to change beginning of rnd, K2tog to end of rnd. 21 (23) sts.
Rnd 11: K all sts.

Finishing

Cut yarn and thread through remaining sts, pull snug and secure.
Weave in ends. Block.

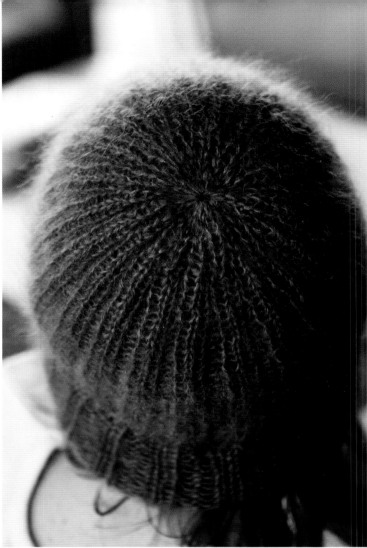

RAIN CHAIN SHAWLETTE

by Michele Lee Bernstein

FINISHED MEASUREMENTS
19" back depth, 57" at widest point, blocked

YARN
Knit Picks Gloss Fingering (70% Merino Wool, 30% Silk; 220 yards/50g): Masala 25013, 2 balls.

NEEDLES
US 4 (3.5mm) straight or circular needles, or size to obtain gauge

NOTIONS
Yarn Needle
3 Stitch Markers
Cable Needle
Size 6/0 Beads, approximately 250 (optional)
US 13/14 (0.90 mm) crochet hook for placing optional beads

GAUGE
16 sts and 32 rows = 4" in Garter stitch, blocked. (Gauge for this project is approximate)

Rain Chain Shawlette

Notes:

The Rain Chain Shawlette is worked flat, from side to side. It features a built in I-cord top edge with a garden "rain chain" detail, garter stitch body, and floral edging. Gradual increases and decreases in the garter stitch section create a graceful crescent curve. Optional beads add the sparkle of raindrops, and weight for drape. When worked in Masala, it calls to mind the traditional Japanese copper rain chain (kusari doi), but you may knit yours in any color to suit your fancy.

The pattern begins with 12 setup rows. Rows 13-36 are repeated, while shaping is made in the Garter Stitch Section. The pattern ends with 12 finishing rows.

All slipped sts are slipped P-wise, WYIF.

Place Bead (PB): Place bead on crochet hook, hook st from LH needle and pull it through bead, replace bead on LH needle and knit it as usual. If you do not wish to use beads, simply work the st. In the Rain Chain section, this st should be knit TBL on rows 23, 25, and 27 if you are not using beads. Some beads are added after RS row st is worked, to be purled on following row, because it is easier to place them while RS row is facing you (K2togPB, SSKPB, KPB).

Garter Section (work Increase, Decrease, or straight with no shaping, as specified in pattern)
Increase Rows (RS): K to last 2 sts of Garter Section, KFB, K1. 1 st inc.
Decrease Rows (RS): K to last 3 sts of Garter Section, K2tog, K1. 1 st dec.
All Other Rows work straight with no shaping, (RS and WS): K all sts.

Chart shows every fourth row as shaded to remind you to increase or decrease in the garter section, and to place beads on the flower edging on these rows. Read the chart on RS rows (odd numbers) from right to left, and on WS rows (even numbers) from left to right.

Markers separate I-cord edging, rain chain detail, garter stitch section, and floral edging. Slip markers as you come to them.

Elastic Bind Off: K2, *insert left needle into fronts of these 2 sts from left to right and K them together TBL (1 st BO), K1; rep from * until 1 st remains. Cut yarn and pull through last st.

K2togPB: K2tog, then place bead on this st to P on next row.
SSKPB: SSK, then place bead on this st to P on next row.
KPB: K st, then place bead on this st to P on next row.

Loop3 (worked over 3 sts): Take third st on left needle, pass it over next 2 sts to the right and drop off needle, K1, YO, K1.

2 ST LPT (2 st left purl twist): Sl 1 to CN, hold in front, P1, K1 TBL from CN.
2 ST RPT (2 st right purl twist): Sl 1 to CN, hold in back, K1 TBL, P1 from CN.

Rain Chain Pattern (worked flat)

Set-up Rows
Row 1 (RS): K1, Sl 1, K1, PM, P2, K3, P2, PM, K2 in Garter Section, PM, YO, K2tog, K1, YO, K1. 17 sts.
Even Rows 2-12 (WS): Sl 1, P to M, Garter Section, K2, P3, K2, Sl 1, K1, Sl 1.
Row 3: K1, Sl 1, K1, P2, Loop3, P2, SM, KFB, K1 in Garter Section, SM, YO, K2tog, YO, SSKPB, YO, K1. 1 st inc, plus Garter Section increase.
Row 5: K1, Sl 1, K1, P2, K1, PB, K1, P2, Garter Section, YO, K2tog, K1, YO, SSK, YO, K1. 1 st inc.
Row 7: K1, Sl 1, K1, P2, Loop3, P2, inc in Garter Section, YO, K2tog, K2, YO, SSKPB, YO, K1. 1 st inc, plus Garter Section increase.
Row 9: K1, Sl 1, K1, P2, K1, PB, K1, P2, Garter Section, YO, K2tog, K3, YO, SSK, YO, K1. 1 st inc.
Row 11: K1, Sl 1, K1, P2, Loop3, P2, inc in Garter Section, YO, K2tog, K4, YO, SSKPB, YO, K1. 1 st inc, plus Garter Section increase, 25 sts total.

Repeat Rows for Increase, Central, and Decrease Sections
Row 13 (RS): K1, Sl 1, K1, P2, K1, PB, K1, P2, Garter Section, YO, K2tog, K5, YO, SSK, YO, K1. 1 st inc.
Rows 14, 16, 18 (WS): Sl 1, P to M, Garter Section, K2, P3, K2, Sl 1, K1, Sl 1.
Row 15: K1, Sl 1, K1, P2, Loop3, P2, inc or dec in Garter Section, YO, K2tog, K6, YO, SSKPB, YO, K1. 1 st inc, plus Garter Section inc or dec 1 st.
Row 17: K1, Sl 1, K1, P2, K1, PB, K1, P2, Garter Section, YO, K2tog, K7, YO, SSK, YO, K1. 1 st inc.
Row 19: K1, Sl 1, K1, P2, Loop3, P2, inc or dec in Garter Section, YO, K2tog, K8, YO, SSKPB, YO, K1. 1 st inc, plus Garter Section inc or dec 1 st.
Row 20: Sl 1, P to M, Garter Section, K2, P3 TBL, K2, Sl 1, K1, Sl 1.
Row 21: K1, Sl 1, K1, P1, 2 ST RPT, K1 TBL, 2 ST LPT, P1, Garter Section, YO, K2tog, K2, K2tog, YO, K1, YO, SSK, K2, YO, SSK, YO, K1. 1 st inc.
Even Rows 22-28 (WS): Sl 1, P to M, Garter Section, (K1, P1 TBL) 3 times, K1, Sl 1, K1, Sl 1.
Row 23: K1, Sl 1, K1, P1, K1 TBL, P1, PB, P1, K1 TBL, P1, inc or dec in Garter Section, YO, K2tog, K1, K2tog, YO, K1, KPB, K1, YO, SSK, K2, YO, SSKPB, YO, K1. 1 st inc, plus Garter Section inc or dec 1 st.
Row 25: K1, Sl 1, K1, P1, K1 TBL, P1, PB, P1, K1 TBL, P1, Garter Section, YO, K2tog, K3, YO, SK2P, YO, K2, (K2tog, YO) twice, K2tog. 1 st dec.
Row 27: K1, Sl 1, K1, P1, K1 TBL, P1, PB, P1, K1 TBL, P1, inc or dec in Garter Section, YO, K2tog, K7, K2tog, YO, K2togPB, YO, K2tog. 1 st dec, plus Garter Section inc or dec 1 st.
Row 29: K1, Sl 1, K1, P1, 2 ST LPT, K1 TBL, 2 ST RPT, P1, Garter Section, YO, K2tog, K6, (K2tog, YO) twice, K2tog. 1 st dec.
Row 30: Rep Row 20.
Row 31: K1, Sl 1, K1, P2, Loop3, P2, inc or dec in Garter Section, YO, K2tog, K5, K2tog, YO, K2togPB, YO, K2tog. 1 st dec, plus Garter Section inc or dec 1 st.
Rows 32, 34, 36 (WS): Sl 1, P to M, Garter Section, K2, P3, K2, Sl 1, K1, Sl 1.
Row 33: K1, Sl 1, K1, P2, K1, PB, K1, P2, Garter Section, YO, K2tog, K4, (K2tog, YO) twice, K2tog. 1 st dec.
Row 35: K1, Sl 1, K1, P2, Loop3, P2, inc or dec in Garter Section,

YO, K2tog, K3, K2tog, YO, K2togPB, YO, K2tog. 1 st dec, plus Garter Section inc or dec 1 st.

End Section

Row 37 (RS): K1, Sl 1, K1, P2, K1, PB, K1, P2, Garter Section, YO, K2tog, K2, (K2tog, YO) twice, K2tog. 1 st dec.

Even Rows 38-48 (WS): Sl 1, P to M, Garter Section, K2, P3, K2, Sl 1, K1, Sl 1.

Row 39: K1, Sl 1, K1, P2, Loop3, P2, dec in Garter Section, YO, K2tog, K1, K2tog, YO, K2togPB, YO, K2tog. 1 st dec, plus Garter Section dec 1 st.

Row 41: K1, Sl 1, K1, P2, K1, PB, K1, P2, Garter Section, YO, K2tog twice, (YO, K2tog) twice. 1 st dec.

Row 43: K1, Sl 1, K1, P2, Loop3, P2, dec in Garter Section, YO, K2tog, K1, K2togPB, YO, K2tog. 1 st dec, plus Garter Section dec 1 st.

Row 45: K1, Sl 1, K1, P2, K1, PB, K1, P2, Garter Section, YO, K2tog twice, YO, K2tog. 1 st dec.

Row 47: K1, Sl 1, K1, P2, Loop3, P2, dec in Garter Section, YO, K2tog, K1, K2tog. 1 st dec, plus Garter Section dec 1 st.

DIRECTIONS

CO 16 sts.

Set-up Section

Work Rows 1 – 12 of Rain Chain Pattern from chart or written directions, increasing in Garter Section on Rows 3, 7, and 11. 25 sts.

Increase Section

Work Rows 13 - 36 eight times, increasing in Garter Section on Rows 15, 19, 23, 27, 31, and 35. 73 sts.

Central Section

Work Rows 13 – 36 once, with no increases or decreases in Garter Section.

Decrease Section

Work Rows 13 – 36 eight times, decreasing in Garter Section on Rows 15, 19, 23, 27, 31, and 35. 25 sts.

End Section

Work Rows 37 – 48 once, decreasing in Garter Section on Rows 39, 43, and 47. 16 sts.

BO all sts using Elastic Bind Off.

Finishing

Weave in ends, wash and block to Finished Measurements.

Rain Chain Chart

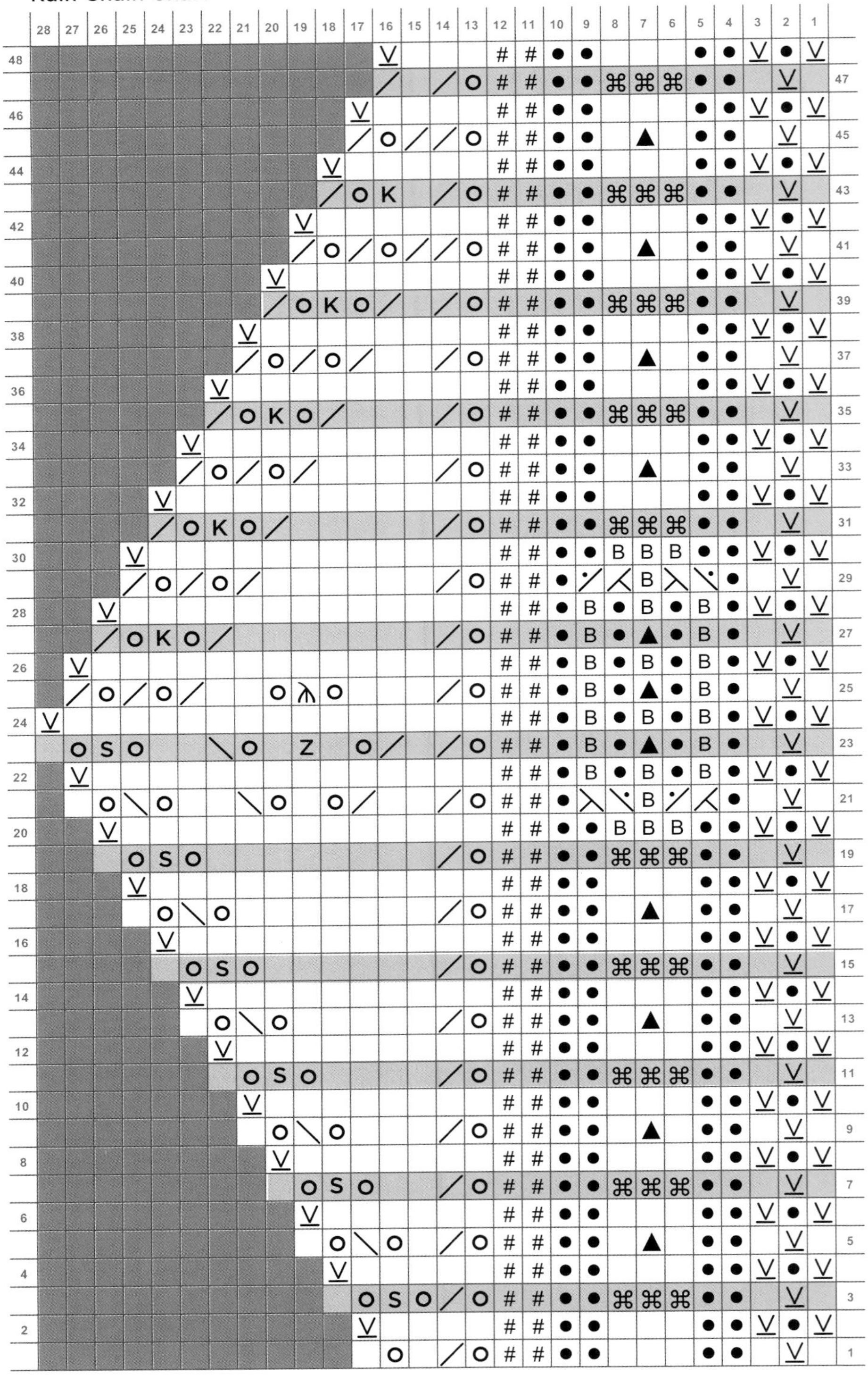

Legend

knit
RS: knit stitch
WS: purl stitch

slip wyif
RS: Slip stitch as if to purl, with yarn in front
WS: Slip stitch as if to purl, with yarn in front

purl
RS: purl stitch
WS: knit stitch

garter section
RS and WS: garter inc/dec section, see notes

yo
RS: Yarn over

k2tog
Knit two stitches together as one stitch

No Stitch
Placeholder - No stitch made.

loop 3
Take 3rd st on left needle, pass it over adjacent 2 sts to the right, drop it off left needle, k1, yo, k1

PB
Place bead then knit st. if not using beads, k this st, or k tbl on Rows 23, 25 and 27.

ssk
Slip one stitch as if to knit, Slip another stitch as if to knit. Insert left-hand needle into front of these 2 stitches and knit them together

knit tbl
RS: Knit stitch through back loop
WS: Purl stitch through back loop

2 st right purl twist
sl1 to CN, hold in back. k1 tbl, p1 from CN

2 st left purl twist
sl1 to CN, hold in front. p1. k1 tbl from CN

sl1 k2tog psso
slip 1, k2tog, pass slip stitch over k2tog

KPB
K st, then place bead on st to work on next row

SSKPB
SSK, then place bead on st to work on next row

K2togPB
K2tog, then place bead on st to work on next row

Chart shows every fourth row as shaded to remind you to increase or decrease in the garter section, and to place beads on the flower edging on these rows. Read the chart on RS rows (odd numbers) from right to left, and on WS rows (even numbers) from left to right.

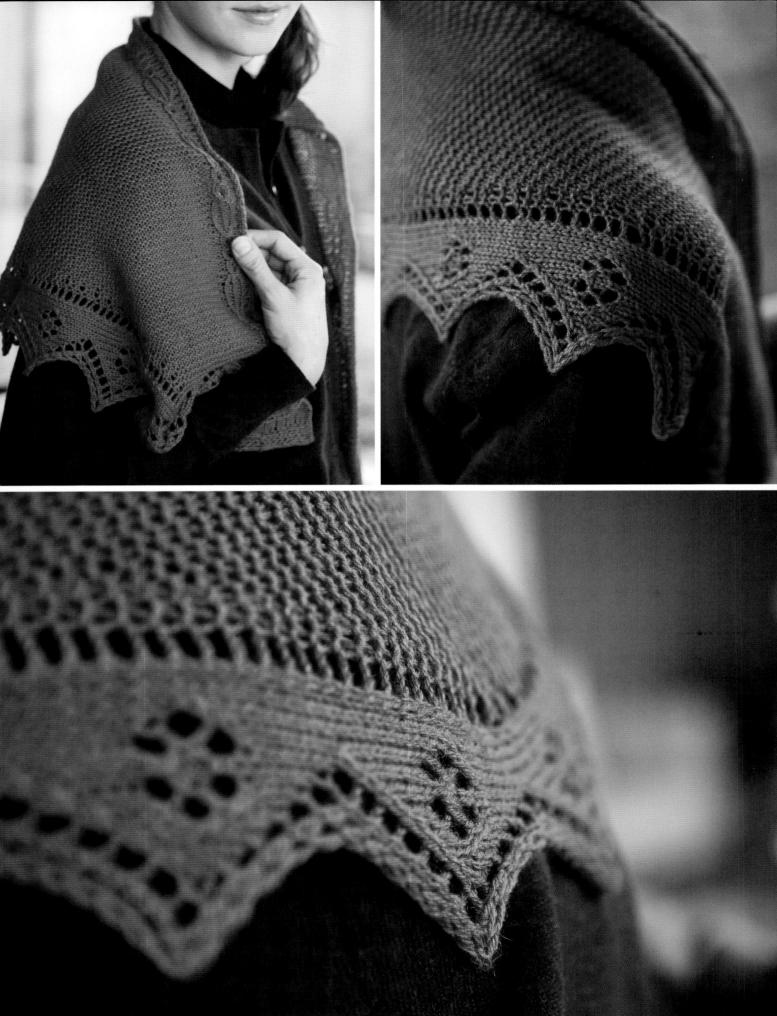

PRAIRIE GOLD

by Kalurah Hudson

FINISHED MEASUREMENTS
5.5" high x 33.25" circumference

YARN
Knit Picks Andean Treasure (100% Baby Alpaca; 110 yards/50g): Prairie Heather 24938, 2 balls.

NEEDLES
US 6 (4mm) 24" circular needles, or size to obtain gauge

NOTIONS
Yarn Needle
Stitch Marker
Cable Needle

GAUGE
24 sts and 24 rounds = 4" in 2 x 2 Rib in the round, blocked.

Prairie Gold

Notes:

This delicate cowl is knit in the round in a unique but simplistic cable pattern. The ribbing flows seamlessly into twisting cables that mimic the swaying of prairie grass.

2/2 LC: Sl 2 sts to CN, hold in front, K2, K2 from CN.

2/2 RC: Sl 2 sts to CN, hold in back, K2, K2 from CN.

2/2 LPC: Sl 2 sts to CN, hold in front, P2, K2 from CN.

2/2 RPC: Sl 2 sts to CN, hold in back, K2, P2 from CN.

2/2/2 LPC: Sl 2 sts to CN, hold in front, K2, P2 over next 4 sts, K2 from CN.

2/2/2 RPC: Sl 4 sts to CN, hold in back, K2 over next 2 sts, P2, K2 from CN.

2 x 2 Rib (worked in the rnd over multiples of 4 sts)
All Rnds: *K2, P2; rep from * to end of rnd.

DIRECTIONS

Loosely CO 200 sts. Join in the rnd and PM, being careful not to twist the sts.

Work Rnds 1-33 from either the Written Instructions below, or the chart. Work each chart row 5 times across the round, reading each row from right to left.

Written Instructions for Cowl, rep each instruction 5 times across the rnd.

Rnds 1 - 8: *K2, P2; rep from * 10 times.

Rnd 9: P4, 2/2 LC, K2, P2, K2, 2/2 RC, P6, 2/2 LC, K2, P2, K2, 2/2 RC, P2.

Rnd 10: P4, K6, P2, K6, P6, *K6, P2; rep from * twice.

Rnd 11: P4, K2, 2/2 LC, P2, 2/2 RC, K2, P6, K2, 2/2 LC, P2, 2/2 RC, K2, P2.

Rnds 12 - 13: Rep Rnd 10.

Rnd 14: P4, 2/2 LPC, K2, P2, K2, 2/2 RPC, P6, 2/2 LPC, K2, P2, K2, 2/2 RPC, P2.

Rnd 15: P6, K4, P2, K4, P10, K4, P2, K4, P4.

Rnd 16: P6, 2/2 LPC, P2, 2/2 RPC, P10, 2/2 LPC, P2, 2/2 RPC, P4.

Rnd 17: P8, K2, P2, K2, P14, K2, P2, K2, P6.

Rnd 18: P8, 2/2/2 LPC, P14, 2/2/2 RPC, P6.

Rnd 19: Rep Rnd 17.

Rnd 20: P6, 2/2 RC, P2, 2/2 LC, P10, 2/2 RC, P2, 2/2 LC, P4.

Rnd 21: Rep Rnd 15.

Rnd 22: P4, 2/2 RC, K2, P2, K2, 2/2 LC, P6, 2/2 RC, K2, P2, K2, 2/2 LC, P2.

Rnd 23: Rep Rnd 10.

Rnd 24: Rep Rnd 10.

Rnd 25: P4, K2, 2/2 RC, P2, 2/2 LC, K2, P6, K2, 2/2 RC, P2, 2/2 LC, K2, P2.

Rnd 26: *K2, (P2, K6) x 2, P2; rep from * twice.

Rnd 27: *K2, P2, 2/2 RPC, K2, P2, K2, 2/2 LPC, P2; rep from * again.

Rnds 28 - 33: *K2, P2; rep from 10 times.

BO in 2 x 2 Rib pattern.

Finishing

Weave in ends, wash and block to Finished Measurements.

Prairie Gold Chart

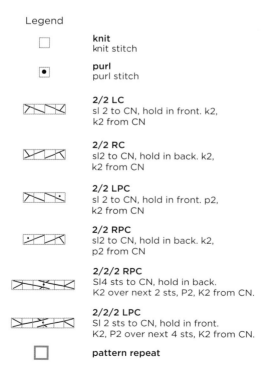

Legend

☐ **knit**
knit stitch

▣ **purl**
purl stitch

2/2 LC
sl 2 to CN, hold in front. k2,
k2 from CN

2/2 RC
sl2 to CN, hold in back. k2,
k2 from CN

2/2 LPC
sl 2 to CN, hold in front. p2,
k2 from CN

2/2 RPC
sl2 to CN, hold in back. k2,
p2 from CN

2/2/2 RPC
Sl4 sts to CN, hold in back.
K2 over next 2 sts, P2, K2 from CN.

2/2/2 LPC
Sl 2 sts to CN, hold in front.
K2, P2 over next 4 sts, K2 from CN.

☐ **pattern repeat**

TOCCATA COWL

by Tetiana Otruta

FINISHED MEASUREMENTS
22" circumference around neck, unstretched; 20" high along center st.

YARN
Knit Picks Alpaca Cloud Fingering (100% Superfine Alpaca; 200 yards/50g): Marianne 26902, 1 hank.

NEEDLES
US 5 (3.75mm) 32" or longer circular needle for Magic Loop technique, or size to obtain gauge.

NOTIONS
Stitch Markers, one of a different color
Yarn Needle

GAUGE
19 sts and 28 rnds = 4" in St st worked flat and in the rnd, relaxed after blocking.

Toccata Cowl

Notes:
This cowl is worked flat until the lace edge, then the lace edge is joined and worked in the round.
Read Chart A from right to left.

DIRECTIONS

Setup Rows (worked flat)
CO 3 sts.
Row 1 (RS): K3.
Row 2 (WS): K1, M1, K1, M1, K1. 5 sts.
Row 3: K2, YO, K1, YO, K2. 7 sts.
Row 4: K2, P3, K2.

Body (worked flat)
Row 1 (RS): K2, PM, YO, K1, YO, PM, K1 (Center st), PM, YO, K1, YO, PM, K2. 11 sts.
Row 2 (WS): K2, P to last M, K2.
Row 3: K2, SM, YO, K to M, YO, SM, K1 (Center st), SM, YO, K to M, YO, SM, K2. 4 sts inc.
Row 4: K2, P to last M, K2.
Rep Rows 3-4 32 more times, until you have 143 sts on needle.

Joining Rnd: SL1, K1, SM, K to M, YO, SM, K1 (Center st), SM, YO, K to M, SM, K1, K2TOG with the first slipped st. 144 sts in the rnd.
Next Rnd: SL1, remove M, K to M, SM, K1 (Center st), SM, K to M, remove M, SK2P with the first slipped st, PM of different color for rnd beginning here. 142 sts.

Rnd 1: K to M, YO, SM, K1 (Center st), SM, YO, K to M. 144 sts.
Rnds 2 and 4: Knit.
Rnd 3: Rep Rnd 1. 146 sts.

Lace Edge (worked in the round) Chart A

If working from the chart, work each pattern repeat 4 times across the rnd.
Rnd 1: *K3, K2TOG, K2, YO, P1, YO, K2, SKP, K4; rep from * to 8 sts from M, K3, K2TOG, K2, YO, P1, YO, SM, K1 (Center st), SM, YO, P1, YO, K2, SKP, K4, **K3, K2TOG, K2, YO, P1, YO, K2, SKP, K4; rep from ** to end of rnd. 2 sts inc.
Rnd 2: *K7, P1, K8; rep from * to 9 sts from M, K7, P1, K1, SM, K1, SM, K1, P1, K8, **K7, P1, K8; rep from ** to end of rnd.
Rnd 3: *K2, K2TOG, K2, YO, K1, P1, K1, YO, K2, SKP, K3; rep from * to 9 sts from M, K2, K2TOG, K2, YO, K1, P1, K1, YO, SM, K1, SM, YO, K1, P1, K1, YO, K2, SKP, K3, **K2, K2TOG, K2, YO, K1, P1, K1, YO, K2, SKP, K3; rep from ** to end of rnd. 2 sts inc.
Rnd 4: *K7, P1, K8; rep from * to 10 sts from M, K7, P1, K2, SM, K1, SM, K2, P1, K8, **K7, P1, K8; rep from ** to end of rnd.
Rnd 5: *K1, K2TOG, K2, YO, K2, P1, K2, YO, K2, SKP, K2; rep from * to 10 sts from M, K1, K2TOG, K2, YO, K2, P1, K2, YO, SM, K1, SM, YO, K2, P1, K2, YO, K2, SKP, K2, **K1, K2TOG, K2, YO, K2, P1, K2, YO, K2, SKP, K2; rep from ** to end of rnd. 2 sts inc.
Rnd 6: *K7, P1, K8; rep from * to 11 sts from M, K7, P1, K3, SM, K1, SM, K3, P1, K8, **K7, P1, K8; rep from ** to end of rnd.
Rnd 7: *K2TOG, K2, YO, K3, P1, K3, YO, K2, SKP, K1; rep from * to 11 sts from M, K2TOG, K2, YO, K3, P1, K3, YO, SM, K1, SM, YO, K3, P1, K3, YO, K2, SKP, K1, **K2TOG, K2, YO, K3, P1, K3, YO, K2, SKP, K1; rep from ** to end of the rnd. 2 sts inc.

Rnd 8: *K7, P1; rep from * to 4 sts from M, K to M, SM, K1, SM, K4, P1, **K7, P1; rep from ** to end of rnd.
Rnd 9: *K3, K2TOG, K2, YO, P1, YO, K2, SKP, K3, P1; rep from * to 12 sts from M, K3, K2TOG, K2, YO, P1, YO, K2, SKP, YO, SM, K1, SM, YO, K2TOG, K2, YO, P1, YO, K2, SKP, K3, P1, **K3, K2TOG, K2, YO, P1, YO, K2, SKP, K3, P1; rep from ** to end of rnd. 2 sts inc.
Rnd 10: *K7, P1; rep from * to 5 sts from M, K to M, SM, K1, SM, K5, P1, **K7, P1; rep from ** to end of rnd.
Rnd 11: *K2, K2TOG, K2, YO, K1, P1, K1, YO, K2, SKP, K2, P1; rep from * to 13 sts from M, K2, K2TOG, K2, YO, K1, P1, K1, YO, K2, SKP, YO, SM, K1, SM, YO, K2TOG, K2, YO, K1, P1, K1, YO, K2, SKP, K2, P1, **K2, K2TOG, K2, YO, K1, P1, K1, YO, K2, SKP, K2, P1; rep from ** to end of rnd. 2 sts inc.
Rnd 12: *K7, P1; rep from * to 6 sts from M, K to M, SM, K1, SM, K6, P1, **K7, P1; rep from ** to end of rnd.
Rnd 13: *K1, K2TOG, K2, YO, K2, P1, K2, YO, K2, SKP, K1, P1; rep from * to 14 sts from M, K1, K2TOG, K2, YO, K2, P1, K2, YO, K2, SKP, YO, SM, K1, SM, YO, K2TOG, K2, YO, K2, P1, K2, YO, K2, SKP, K1, P1, **K1, K2TOG, K2, YO, K2, P1, K2, YO, K2, SKP, K1, P1; rep from ** to end of rnd. 2 sts inc.
Rnd 14: *K7, P1; rep from * to 7 sts from M, K to M, SM, K1, SM, **K7, P1; rep from ** to end of rnd.
Rnd 15: *K2TOG, K2, YO, K3, P1, K3, YO, K2, SKP, P1; rep from * to 15 sts from M, K2TOG, K2, YO, K3, P1, K3, YO, K2, SKP, YO, SM, K1, SM, YO, K2TOG, K2, YO, K3, P1, K3, YO, K2, SKP, P1, **K2TOG, K2, YO, K3, P1, K3, YO, K2, SKP, P1; rep from ** to end of rnd. 2 sts inc.
Rnd 16: *K7, P1; rep from * to M, SM, K1, SM, P1, **K7, P1; rep from ** to end of rnd.
Rnd 17: *YO, K2, SKP, K3, P1, K3, K2TOG, K2, YO, P1; rep from * to M, YO, SM, K1, SM, YO, P1, **YO, K2, SKP, K3, P1, K3, K2TOG, K2, YO, P1; rep from ** to end of rnd. 2 sts inc.
Rnd 18: *K7, P1; rep from * to 1 st from M, K1, SM, K1, SM, K1, P1, **K7, P1; rep from ** to end of rnd.
Rnd 19: *K1, YO, K2, SKP, K2, P1, K2, K2TOG, K2, YO, K1, P1; rep from * to 1 st from M, K1, YO, SM, K1, SM, YO, K1, P1, **K1, YO, K2, SKP, K2, P1, K2, K2TOG, K2, YO, K1, P1; rep from ** to end of rnd. 2 sts inc.
Rnd 20: *K7, P1; rep from * to 2 sts from M, K2, SM, K1, SM, K2, P1, **K7, P1; rep from ** to end of rnd.
Rnd 21: *K2, YO, K2, SKP, K1, P1, K1, K2TOG, K2, YO, K2, P1; rep from * to 2 sts from M, K2, YO, SM, K1, SM, YO, K2, P1, **K2, YO, K2, SKP, K1, P1, K1, K2TOG, K2, YO, K2, P1; rep from ** to end of rnd. 2 sts inc.
Rnd 22: *K7, P1; rep from * to 3 sts from M, K3, SM, K1, SM, K3, P1, **K7, P1; rep from ** to end of rnd.
Rnd 23: *K3, YO, K2, SKP, P1, K2TOG, K2, YO, K3, P1; rep from * to 3 sts from M, K3, YO, SM, K1, SM, YO, K3, P1, **K3, YO, K2, SKP, P1, K2TOG, K2, YO, K3, P1; rep from ** to end of rnd. 2 sts inc.
Rnd 24: *K7, P1; rep from * to 4 sts from M, K4, SM, K1, SM, K4, P1, **K7, P1; rep from ** to end of rnd.
Rnd 25: *YO, K2, SKP, YO, K1, SKP, P1, K2TOG, K1, YO, K2TOG, K2, YO, P1; rep from * to 4 st from M, YO, K2, SKP, YO, SM, K1, SM, YO, K2TOG, K2, YO, P1, **YO, K2, SKP, YO, K1, SKP, P1, K2TOG, K1, YO, K2TOG, K2, YO, P1; rep from ** to end of rnd. 2 sts inc.
Rnd 26: *K7, P1; rep from * to 5 sts from M, K5, SM, K1, SM, K5, P1, **K7, P1; rep from ** to end of rnd.

Chart A

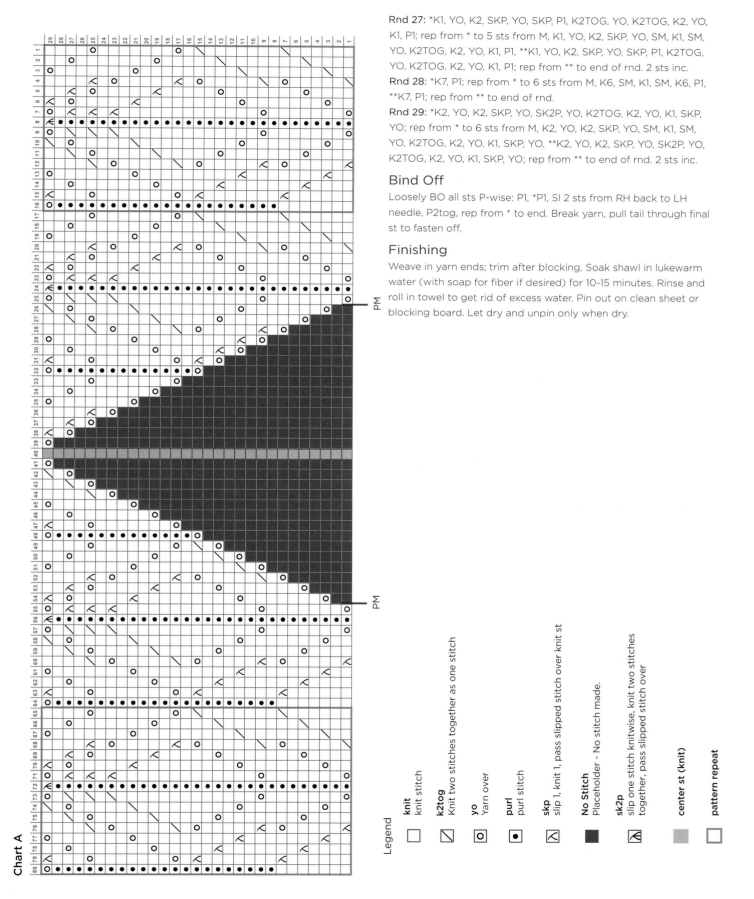

Rnd 27: *K1, YO, K2, SKP, YO, SKP, P1, K2TOG, YO, K2TOG, K2, YO, K1, P1; rep from * to 5 sts from M, K1, YO, K2, SKP, YO, SM, K1, SM, YO, K2TOG, K2, YO, K1, P1, **K1, YO, K2, SKP, YO, SKP, P1, K2TOG, YO, K2TOG, K2, YO, K1, P1; rep from ** to end of rnd. 2 sts inc.

Rnd 28: *K7, P1; rep from * to 6 sts from M, K6, SM, K1, SM, K6, P1, **K7, P1; rep from ** to end of rnd.

Rnd 29: *K2, YO, K2, SKP, YO, SK2P, YO, K2TOG, K2, YO, K1, SKP, YO; rep from * to 6 sts from M, K2, YO, K2, SKP, YO, SM, K1, SM, YO, K2TOG, K2, YO, K1, SKP, YO, **K2, YO, K2, SKP, YO, SK2P, YO, K2TOG, K2, YO, K1, SKP, YO; rep from ** to end of rnd. 2 sts inc.

Bind Off

Loosely BO all sts P-wise: P1, *P1, Sl 2 sts from RH back to LH needle, P2tog, rep from * to end. Break yarn, pull tail through final st to fasten off.

Finishing

Weave in yarn ends; trim after blocking. Soak shawl in lukewarm water (with soap for fiber if desired) for 10-15 minutes. Rinse and roll in towel to get rid of excess water. Pin out on clean sheet or blocking board. Let dry and unpin only when dry.

Legend

knit
knit stitch

k2tog
Knit two stitches together as one stitch

yo
Yarn over

purl
purl stitch

skp
slip 1, knit 1, pass slipped stitch over knit st

No Stitch
Placeholder - No stitch made.

sk2p
slip one stitch knitwise, knit two stitches together, pass slipped stitch over

center st (knit)

pattern repeat

TARGET BERET

by Violet LeBeaux

FINISHED MEASUREMENTS
20" brim circumference, 8.5" brim to top of stem, 10" flat diameter

YARN
Knit Picks Reverie Worsted (80% Baby Alpaca, 20% Acrylic; 137 yards/50g): MC Natural 26113, C1 Silver 26581, 1 skein each

NEEDLES
US 6 (4mm) DPNs or long circular needles for Magic Loop technique, or size to obtain gauge

NOTIONS
Yarn Needle
Stitch Marker

GAUGE
22 sts and 28 rows = 4" in St st in the round, blocked.
20 sts and 28 rows = 4" in stranded ribbing in the round, blocked.

Target Beret

Notes:

This is a sweetly feminine beret knit in the round that takes advantage of the drape and halo of lovely alpaca yarn. The beret is knit in the round from brim to tip and features a striped rib brim and a concentric circle design achieved by switching colors at the beginning of each stripe so the colors are carried up the inside.

DIRECTIONS

Brim

With MC, CO 100 sts, PM and join being careful not to twist.

Rnds 1-7: *With MC, K2, with C1, P2; rep from * to end of rnd.

Body

Rnd 8: With MC, *K2, M1; rep from * to end of rnd. 150 sts.

Rnds 9-10: K to end.

Rnds 11-13: With C1, K to end.

Rnds 14-16: With MC, K to end.

Rnds 17-28: Rep Rnds 11-16 two more times.

Rnds 29-31: With C1, K to end.

Rnd 32: With MC, *K4, K2tog; rep from * until less than 6 sts remain, K to end. 125 sts.

Rnds 33-34: K to end.

Rnd 35: With C1, *K4, K2tog; rep from * until less than 6 sts remain, K to end. 105 sts.

Rnds 36-37: K to end.

Rnds 38-55: Rep Rnds 32-37 three more times. 37 sts.

Rnds 56-58: Rep Rnds 32-34 once more. 31 sts.

Rnd 59: With C1, *K1, K2tog; rep from * until 1 st remains, K1. 21 sts.

Rnd 60: *K1, K2tog; rep from * to end. 14 sts.

Rnd 61: *K1, K2tog; rep from * until 2 sts remain, K2. 10 sts.

Stem

Rnd 62: With MC, *K1, K2tog; rep from * until 1 st remains, K1. 7 sts.

Rnds 63-70: K to end.

There should be a total of 19 colored stripes after the brim including stem.

BO by passing yarn through remaining 7 sts and pulling tight.

Finishing

Secure and weave in ends, wash and block to Finished Measurements.

OSTREO SHAWLETTE

by Joyce Fassbender

FINISHED MEASUREMENTS
50" wide x 25" long

YARN
Knit Picks Alpaca Cloud Fingering (100% Superfine Alpaca; 200 yards/50g): Elinor 26914, 2 skeins.

NEEDLES
US 5 (3.75mm) 24" circular needles, or size to obtain gauge

NOTIONS
Yarn Needle
Stitch Markers

GAUGE
22 sts and 28 rows = 4" over lace patterns, blocked.

Ostreo Shawlette

Notes:

This is a triangle shawlette worked from the center back down to the bottom edge. Increases are worked at the ends of each row and the center stitch to give the shawl its triangular shape.

All rows are worked with two edge stitches in garter stitch. These stitches, as well as the center stitch and WS rows, are not included on the charts.

In order to change the size of the shawl, work one or more additional repeats of Chart B. Each additional repeat will result in an increase of 40 stitches per side.

Use stitch markers at center stitch and between stitch pattern repeats if necessary. Stitch markers between stitch pattern repeats will need to be repositioned between charts. Boxed areas of charts indicate the pattern repeat across rows. Please see instructions below for additional information.

K2tog Bind Off

K2, SL 2 sts onto left needle, K2tog TBL, *K1, SL 2 sts onto left needle, K2tog TBL*, rep sts between * until all sts are bound off. Break yarn and pull through final st to fasten off.

DIRECTIONS

CO 5 sts using a Long Tail cast on.

Set up rows:
Row 1: K1, M1, K3, M1, K1. 7 sts.
Row 2: K all sts.

Work Charts

Odd (RS) rows are charted and worked right to left as: K2 (edge stitches), work chart, K1 (center stitch), work chart again, K2 (edge stitches).

Even (WS) rows are not included on the charts and should be worked as: K2, P to last 2 sts, K2.

Work Chart 1 once. 55 sts.

Work Chart 2 twice. Rep boxed area of stitch pattern repeat two times per side for first chart repeat, then 6 times per side for second chart repeat. Move stitch markers between stitch pattern repeats one stitch to the left on Rows 5, 9, 13, and 19. 215 sts.

Work Chart 3 once. Rep boxed area of stitch pattern repeat 10 times per side. Move stitch markers between stitch pattern repeats one stitch to the left on Rows 5, 9, and 13. 255 sts.

Work Chart 4 once. Rep boxed area of stitch pattern repeat 12 times per side. Move stitch markers between stitch pattern repeats one stitch to the left on Row 7. 371 sts.

Finishing

BO all sts using the K2tog Bind Off. Weave in ends. Block to finished measurements.

Chart 1

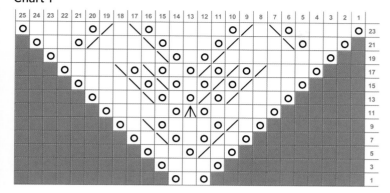

Legend

■	**No Stitch**	Placeholder - No stitch made.
⊡	**yo**	Yarn over
□	**knit**	knit stitch
╱	**k2tog**	Knit two stitches together as one stitch
⋏	**sl1, k2tog, psso**	Slip one stitch, k2tog, pass slipped stitch over k2tog
╲	**ssk**	Slip one stitch as if to knit, slip another stitch as if to knit. Insert left-hand needle into front of these 2 stitches and knit them together
⋀	**Central Double Dec**	Slip first and second stitches together as if to knit. Knit 1 stitch. Pass two slipped stitches over the knit stitch.
□	**pattern repeat**	

Chart 2

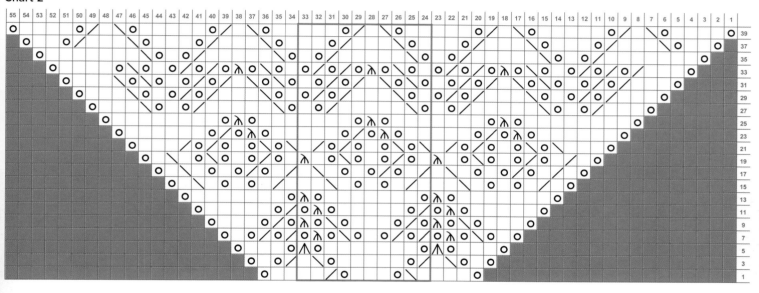

Chart 3

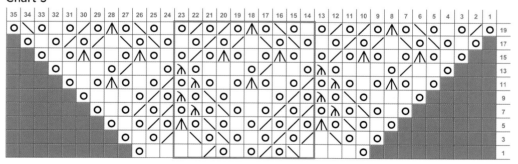

Chart 4

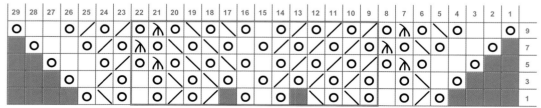

RIQUE RAQUE SCARF

by Patricia Duncan

FINISHED MEASUREMENTS
10 x 55"

YARN
Knit Picks Luminance (100% Silk; 439 yards/50g): Thoughtful 27049, 1 hank

NEEDLES
US 3 (3.25mm) 10" straight or 16" circular needles, or size to obtain gauge
US 2 (2.75mm) DPNs, or one size smaller than size to obtain gauge

NOTIONS
Yarn Needle
Stitch Markers
Scrap Yarn for provisional cast-on
Crochet Hook, size G, or any size that will hold scrap yarn
Blocking Wires

GAUGE
24 sts and 36 rows = 4" over Little Vine lace pattern on larger needles, blocked. (Gauge for this project is approximate.)

Rique Raque Scarf

Notes:

This scarf was inspired by the rick rack trimming my mother used to sew onto my skirts and blouses when I was a kid. It begins with a provisional crochet cast-on using scrap yarn, then the garment is knitted from side to side in rows. When the desired length is reached, the eyelet edging is knitted from side to side in rows and attached to the narrow ends. Blocking the finished piece creates lightly zigzagged edges all around, which subtly echo the main motif of the center section.

The center section of the scarf is charted; the edging is presented both in words and in chart form. Work the charts from right to left on RS rows (odd numbers) and left to right on WS rows (even numbered).

Eyelet Edging Pattern (worked flat)
Row 1 (RS): Sl1 WYIF, K1, YO, K2tog, YO twice, K1.
Row 2 (WS): Sl1 WYIB, (K1, P1) in double YO, K1, YO, K2tog, K last st together with 1 st from center section TBL.
Row 3: Sl1 WYIF, K1, YO, K2tog, K3.
Row 4: BO 2 sts knitwise, K1, YO, K2tog, K last st together with 1 st from center section TBL.
Rep Rows 1-4 for pattern.

DIRECTIONS

Center Section
The center section is worked flat from end to end. It consists of 3 panels, a center panel of Little Vine Lace bordered on both sides by panels of Honeycomb Lace.

Set-Up
With the crochet hook and scrap yarn, make a chain about 60 sts long. Cut yarn and pull thread through final loop. Using the larger of the knitting needles and main yarn, pick up 56 sts in the purl bumps along the chain.
Purl 1 row, increasing 5 sts evenly spaced. 61 sts.

Work Row 1 of Center Section Chart. PM between the Honeycomb borders and the Little Vine Lace; if desired, PM between each of the Little Vine reps. You may like to use different colored markers to separate the Honeycomb borders from the Little Vine Lace reps.
Complete Rows 1-8 of the chart 56 times, slipping markers as you come to them. Then work Rows 1-7 once.
Purl 1 row, decreasing 5 sts evenly spaced. 56 sts. Cut yarn.

Edging
The edging is worked flat on the smaller DPNs. It is joined to the center section on WS Rows 2 and 4 by knitting the final st of the Edging row together with a live center st TBL.

Set Up
Hold the center section with the WS facing. If you are using a circular needle for the Center Section, a point protector may help secure the LH end of the needle. If you are using a set of straight needles, slide the live sts from the working needle onto the second needle so the point is aligned to the right.

Cast 5 sts onto the DPN and knit 1 row up to the final st. K this last st together with the first WS center st TBL, joining the edging and center together.

Turn and work RS Row 1 of the edging, following either the Eyelet Edging Chart or the written instructions above. Note that, after binding off 2 sts on Row 4, you will have one st remaining on the RH needle, four on the LH needle.
Continuing in this manner, work 27 reps of the edging.
Turn. Sl1 WYIF, K remaining sts. Turn.
BO 4 sts. K final st of edging together with final st of center section TBL.
Cut yarn, thread through a yarn needle, and pull through the loop. Weave working yarn tail invisibly along the WS joining row between the center section and the edging.

Remove provisional CO from opposite end of scarf, slipping each live st onto the larger needle as it is released. Rep Eyelet edging to correspond to other end.

Finishing
Soak the finished scarf thoroughly in a basin of cool water. Squeeze gently to remove water and lay out on a blocking mat. On the long edges, weave blocking wires through the row of holes formed by the honeycomb sts. To gently scallop the edge, weave the wire through each hole from front to back. In the same manner, weave wires through each hole of the eyelet edging on the short ends. Stretch and pin to measurements.
Allow to dry thoroughly before removing wires and pins. Weave in yarn ends. Cut threads.

Center Section Chart

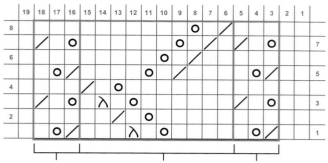

	19	18	17	16	15	14	13	12	11	10	9	8	7	6	5	4	3	2	1	
8												O		/						
			/	O						O				/		O				7
6										O										
			O	/				O							O	/				5
4							O					/								
				O	/	λ		O							O					3
2						/	O													
			O	/		λ	O						O	/						1

Honeycomb rep sts 16-18 three times

Little Vine Lace rep sts 6-15 four times

Honeycomb rep sts 3-5 three times

Eyelet Edging Chart

	7	6	5	4	3	2	1	
4	◠	◠	●	●	O	/	Ω	
					/	O	V	3
2	V	●		●	O	/	Ω	
			O	O	/	O	V	1

Note: For the Eyelet Edging chart only, work the / as k2 tog on both RS and WS rows. Bind-offs on row 4 are also knitted. St 5 on Row 4 rem on RH needle after the bind-off.

Legend

knit
RS: knit stitch
WS: purl stitch

k2tog
RS: Knit two stitches together as one stitch
WS: Purl 2 stitches together

bind off
RS: Bind off a stitch by knitting 2 stitches, then passing the first stitch over the second.
WS: Bind off a stitch by purling 2 stitches, then passing the first stitch over the second.

sl1 k psso
slip 1, knit 1, pass slipped stitch over knit 1

slip wyif
RS: Slip stitch as if to purl, with yarn in front
WS: Slip stitch as if to purl, with yarn in back

yo
Yarn over

join 1 edging st to1 center st
WS: With LH needle, pick up one st from the center panel. Sl1 st from edging onto the LH needle, then p2tog tbl.

purl
RS: purl stitch
WS: knit stitch

QUEENSWAY SHAWL

by Holli Yeoh

FINISHED MEASUREMENTS

22" wide x 78" long

YARN

Knit Picks Aloft (72% Super Kid Mohair, 28% Silk; 260 yards/25g): Cosmopolitan 25212, 4 balls

NEEDLES

US 8 (5mm) straight or 16-24" circular needles, or size to obtain gauge
US 6 (4mm) 60" circular needle, or 2 sizes smaller than needle to obtain gauge

NOTIONS

180 6/0 beads, Silver 81611
Size E-4 (3.5mm) Crochet Hook and Waste Yarn, or preferred method for provisional cast on
0.6mm Crochet Hook (for placing beads)
Yarn Needle
Stitch Markers

GAUGE

14 sts and 23 rows = 4" in St st with larger needles, blocked

Queensway Shawl

Notes:

Tuck stitches create a diamond motif over a ground of reverse stockinette stitch. All of the fancy stitch work is done on WS rows (on the knit side), alternating with a rest row on the RS. Beads are placed where needed using a small crochet hook. Stitches are picked up around the perimeter and a narrow band of eyelets is worked before knitting on a perpendicular lace edging. The ends of the lace edging are grafted together where they meet. Be aware that on the Diamond Chart, the blank square indicates a purl stitch on the RS and knit stitch on the WS.

Provisional Crochet Cast On

With waste yarn, make a slip knot and insert larger crochet hook. Holding hook in dominant hand and knitting needle in the other, *bring working yarn behind needle and with hook, reach over top of needle and crochet a chain st thus wrapping yarn around needle; rep from * until desired number of sts are cast on. Work a few more chain sts (not around knitting needle) and fasten off.

Tuck Stitch (T2 and T4)

Tuck 2 (T2): Knit into st 2 rows below next st on needle. Drop LH st off needle and encourage sts to unravel.

Tuck 4 (T4): Knit into st 4 rows below next st on needle. Drop LH st off needle and encourage sts to unravel. Alternatively, drop next st off LH needle, unravel 4 rows and knit into st 4 rows below dropped st.

Place Bead (PB)

Slip bead onto small crochet hook. Slip hook into next st K-wise and slide bead onto st. Transfer st back to left needle and then knit st.

Reverse Stockinette Stitch (Rev St st)

Row 1 (RS): Purl.
Row 2 (WS): Knit.
Rep Rows 1-2 for pattern.

The Diamond and Edging Patterns can be worked from either the charts, or written instructions below. If using the charts, read RS rows (odd numbers from right to left, and WS rows from left to right.

Diamond Pattern (worked flat over 43 sts)

Row 1 and all RS rows: Purl.
Row 2 (WS): K21, T2, K21.
Row 4: K20, T2, K1, T2, K20.
Row 6: K19, (T2, K1) twice, T2, K19.
Row 8: K18, (T2, K1) 3 times, T2, K18.
Row 10: K17, T2, K1, T2, K3, T2, K1, T2, K17.
Row 12: K16, T2, K1, T2, K5, T2, K1, T2, K16.
Row 14: K15, T2, K1, T2, K7, T2, K1, T2, K15.
Row 16: K14, T2, K1, T2, K4, PB, K4, T2, K1, T2, K14.
Row 18: K13, T2, K1, T2, K11, T2, K1, T2, K13.
Row 20: K12, T2, K1, T2, K4, PB, K1, T4, K1, PB, K4, T2, K1, T2, K12.
Row 22: K11, T2, K1, T2, K15, T2, K1, T2, K11.
Row 24: K10, T2, K1, T2, K4, (PB, K1, T4, K1) twice, PB, K4, T2, K1, T2, K10.
Row 26: K9, T2, K1, T2, K19, T2, K1, T2, K9.

Row 28: K8, T2, K1, T2, K6, (T4, K1, PB, K1) twice, T4, K6, T2, K1, T2, K8.
Row 30: K7, (T2, K1) twice, T2, K19, (T2, K1) twice, T2, K7.
Row 32: K6, (T2, K1) 3 times, T2, K6, T4, K1, PB, K1, T4, K6, (T2, K1) 3 times, T2, K6.
Row 34: K5, T2, K1, T2, K3, T2, K1, T2, K15, T2, K1, T2, K3, T2, K1, T2, K5.
Row 36: K4, T2, K1, T2, K5, T2, K1, T2, K6, T4, K6, T2, K1, T2, K5, T2, K1, T2, K4.
Row 38: K3, T2, K1, T2, K7, T2, K1, T2, K11, T2, K1, T2, K7, T2, K1, T2, K3.
Row 40: K2, (T2, K1, T2, K9) 3 times, T2, K1, T2, K2.
Row 42: (K1, T2) twice, K11, T2, K1, T2, K7, T2, K1, T2, K11, (T2, K1) twice.
Row 44: T2, K1, T2, K6, PB, K6, T2, K1, T2, K5, T2, K1, T2, K6, PB, K6, T2, K1, T2.
Row 46: K1, T2, K15, T2, K7, T2, K15, T2, K1.
Row 48: T2, K1, T2, K4, PB, K1, T4, K1, PB, K4, T2, K1, T2, K5, T2, K1, T2, K4, PB, K1, T4, K1, PB, K4, T2, K1, T2.
Row 50: K1, T2, K15, T2, K7, T2, K15, T2, K1.
Row 52: T2, K1, T2, K4, T4, K1, PB, K1, T4, K4, T2, K1, T2, K5, T2, K1, T2, K4, T4, K1, PB, K1, T4, K4, T2, K1, T2.
Row 54: Rep Row 50.
Row 56: T2, K1, T2, K6, T4, K6, T2, K1, T2, K5, T2, K1, T2, K6, T4, K6, T2, K1, T2.
Row 58: Rep Row 42.
Row 60: K2, T2, K1, T2, K9, T2, K1, T2, K4, PB, K4, T2, K1, T2, K9, T2, K1, T2, K2.
Row 62: Rep Row 38.
Row 64: K4, T2, K1, T2, K5, T2, K1, T2, K4, PB, K1, T4, K1, PB, K4, T2, K1, T2, K5, T2, K1, T2, K4.
Row 66: Rep Row 34.
Row 68: K6, (T2, K1) 3 times, T2, K4, (PB, K1, T4, K1) twice, PB, K4, (T2, K1) 3 times, T2, K6.
Row 70: Rep Row 30.
Row 72: Rep Row 28.
Row 74: Rep Row 26.
Row 76: K10, T2, K1, T2, K6, T4, K1, PB, K1, T4, K6, T2, K1, T2, K10.
Row 78: Rep Row 22.
Row 80: K12, T2, K1, T2, K6, T4, K6, T2, K1, T2, K12.
Row 82: Rep Row 18.
Row 84: K14, T2, K1, T2, K9, T2, K1, T2, K14.
Row 86: Rep Row 14.
Row 88: Rep Row 12.
Row 90: Rep Row 10.
Row 92: Rep Row 8.
Row 94: Rep Row 6.
Row 96: Rep Row 4.
Row 98: Rep Row 2.

Edging Pattern (worked flat, begin with 6 sts)

Stitch count of edging changes from row to row.
Edging is joined to shawl at the end of every WS row with a K2TOG, working last edging st together with next shawl st.
Row 1: Sl 1 WYIF, K1, YO, K2TOG, YO, K2. 7 sts.
Row 2: K6, K2TOG (knit last edging st together with next shawl st).

Row 3: Sl 1 WYIF, K2, YO, K2TOG, YO, K2. 8 sts.
Row 4: K7, K2TOG.
Row 5: Sl 1 WYIF, K3, YO, K2TOG, YO, K2. 9 sts.
Row 6: K8, K2TOG.
Row 7: Sl 1 WYIF, K4, YO, K2TOG, YO, K2. 10 sts.
Row 8: K9, K2TOG.
Row 9: Sl 1 WYIF, K5, YO, K2TOG, YO, K2. 11 sts.
Row 10: BO 5, K5 (include last st remaining from BO in your st count), K2TOG. 6 sts.

DIRECTIONS
Shawl
With waste yarn, larger needles and crochet hook, using Provisional Crochet Cast On method, CO 59 sts.
Beginning with a RS purl row, work 22 rows of Rev St st, ending with a WS knit row.

Begin Diamond Pattern
Row 1 (RS): P8, PM, work Row 1 of Diamond Pattern, PM, P8.
Row 2 (WS): K8, SM, work Row 2 of Diamond Pattern, SM, K8.
Continue as established, working edge sts in Rev St st and Diamond Pattern through Row 72.
Rep Rows 29 to 72 an additional 7 times.
Work Rows 73 to 98 once.
Work 22 rows in Rev St st, ending with a WS knit row.

Setup for Edging
Sts are worked in one piece using the circular needle around the whole perimeter of the shawl. Live sts from the provisional CO and the last row of the shawl are used along with sts picked up along the two long selvedge edges.
Using smaller size circular needle, K2, PM, K to last 2 sts, PM, K2.
Working along left edge of shawl, PU and K2, PM, PU and K220 (working into every other row along the side), PM, PU and K2. Carefully remove provisional CO and transfer sts to empty needle. 58 sts.
Continuing with circular needle, work across CO sts; K2, PM, K to last st, PM, KFB.
Working along right edge of shawl, PU and K2, PM, PU and K220, PM, PU and K2. 566 sts. (Each corner is identified by 4 sts between 2 corner markers. 220 sts between markers on the long edges and 55 sts between markers on the short edges.)
Join to work in the rnd.
Purl 1 rnd, ending at 8th marker (2 sts short of full rnd). This is now the end of rnd marker.
Eyelet Rnd: *K2, YO, K3, (YO, K2TOG) to next marker, K2, YO, K2, (YO, K2TOG) to next marker; rep from * once more. 570 sts; 5 sts between corner markers.

Purl 1 rnd. Break yarn.

Begin Edging Pattern
The edging is joined to the shawl on the WS rows by knitting the last st of the edging row together with the next shawl st on the circular needle.
Using Provisional Crochet Cast On method, CO 6 sts on end of working needle; turn to WS, K6; turn.
Row 1 (RS): K2, YO, K2TOG, YO, K2. 7 edging sts.
Row 2 (WS): K6, knit last edging st together with next shawl st; turn.

Work Rows 3 to 10 of Edging Pattern, then work 43 full reps (Rows 1 to 10) more to corner marker.

Turn Corner
To turn the corner, Edging Pattern is joined to main piece every other WS row as follows, resulting in 2 full reps of Edging Pattern worked over the 5 sts between corner markers:
Work next 3 rows in pattern.
Non-Joining Row (WS): Knit to end of edging sts in pattern (do not join); turn.
Rep last 4 rows to next marker, working Non-Joining Row on Rows 4, 8, 2, 6, and 10 of Edging Pattern.

Continue to work Edging Pattern around the rest of the perimeter, working 11 reps on the short sides, 44 reps on the long side, and 2 reps at the corners as before, ending final corner rep with Row 9.
Last Row (WS): BO 5 sts, graft beginning and end of edging together using sts from provisional CO as a guide. Remove provisional CO.

Finishing
Weave in ends. Wash and block to measurements.

Diamond Chart

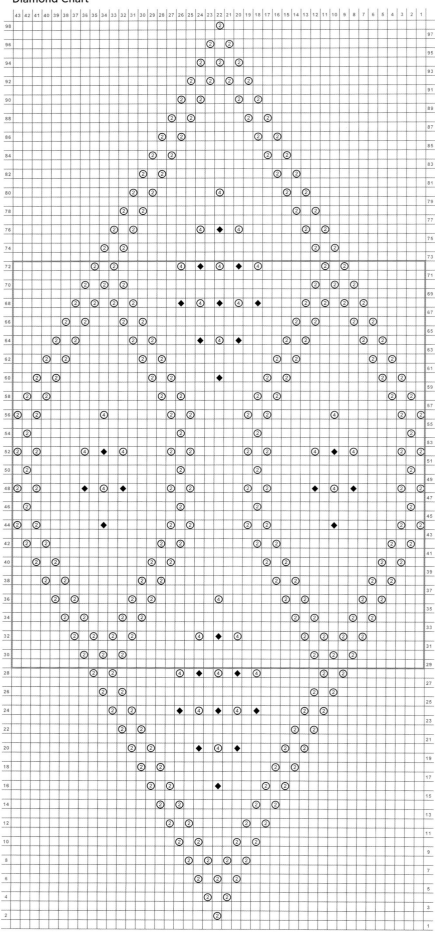

Legend

purl
RS: purl stitch
WS: knit stitch

Ⓩ **T2**
tuck 2 sts below

◆ **PB**
place bead

④ **T4**
tuck 4 sts below

pattern repeat

slip wyif
RS: Slip stitch as if to purl,
with yarn in front

○ **yo**
RS: Yarn Over

╱ **k2tog**
RS: Knit two stitches together
as one stitch

╱ **k2tog edge st**
WS: knit last edging stitch
together with next shawl stitch

No Stitch
Placeholder - No stitch
made.

• **knit**
RS: knit stitch

⌢ **bind off**

Edging Chart

SEPTAFLEUR BERET

by Jennie Santopietro

FINISHED MEASUREMENTS

10.25 (11.5)" diameter, measured flat after blocking; 18 (20)" stretchy brim circumference. To fit head circumferences of 18-22" (22-24").

YARN

Knit Picks Alpaca Cloud Fingering (100% Superfine Alpaca; 200 yards/50g): Mary 26892, 1 (2) hanks

NEEDLES

US 2.5 (3mm) DPN's, plus 16" circular needles, or two 24" circular needles for two circulars technique, or one 32" or longer circular needle for Magic Loop technique, or size to obtain gauge

US 1 (2.25mm) 16" circular needles, or two 24" circular needles for two circulars technique, or one 32" or longer circular needle for Magic Loop technique, or three sizes smaller than needle to obtain gauge

NOTIONS

Yarn Needle
Stitch Markers
Size E Crochet Hook, for CO

GAUGE

28 sts and 48 rows = 4" in Seed stitch with larger needles, blocked

Septafleur Beret

Notes:

This beret is worked from the top down, beginning with a circular cast on technique. Instructions are provided charted and written for your convenience. The flower motif at the crown dissolves into seed stitch as each petal tapers to a point and the piece is finished off with 1x1 Rib on smaller needles for a snug and cozy fit.

Circular Cast On Tutorial: http://tutorials.knitpicks.com/wptutorials/circular-cast-on/.

Seed Stitch (in the rnd over an odd number of sts)
Rnd 1: (K1, P1) to last st, K1.
Rnd 2: (P1, K1) to last st, P1.
Rep Rnds 1-2 for pattern.

1 x 1 Rib (in the rnd over an even number of sts)
All Rnds: (P1, K1) to end.

Simply Stretchy Bind Off
Continue to work in 1x1 Rib pattern. Begin by purling the first st then continue as follows:
Step 1: K1, insert left needle tip into the front of the 2 sts on the right needle, K2tog (1 st on right needle).
Step 2: P1, insert left needle tip into the back of the 2 sts on right needle, P2tog (1 st on right needle).
Rep Steps 1 & 2 until 1 st remains. Break yarn and pull through the final loop to secure.

DIRECTIONS

Size 11.5": Work Rnds 1-81 from Septafleur Combined Chart or Combined Written Instructions, as you prefer.
Size 10.25": Work Rnds 1-8, 11-37, 42-61, 64-79 of Septafleur Combined Chart or Combined Written Instructions, bearing in mind that the 10.25" size has 4 fewer sts per section rep after Rnd 37 (28 fewer sts per rnd).

Combined Written Instructions
Using larger DPNs and the circular cast on method, CO 7 sts. Divide sts onto three DPNs.
Rnd 1: K1 TBL to end.
Rnd 2: KFB to end. 14 sts.
Rnd 3: K even.
Rnd 4: (K1, YO, K1) to end. 21 sts.
Rnds 5-6: K even.
Rnd 7: (K1, YO, K1, YO, K1) to end. 35 sts.
Rnds 8-10: K even. Size 10.25" omit Rnds 9-10.
Rnd 11: (K5, YO) to end. 42 sts.
Rnd 12 and all even numbered rnds through 30: K even.
Rnd 13: (K2, YO, K1, YO, K2, Sl 1 P-wise WYIB) to end. 56 sts.
Rnd 15: (K7, Sl 1 P-wise) to end.
Rnd 17: (K3, YO, K1, YO, K3, Sl 1 P-wise) to end. 70 sts.
Rnd 19: (K9, Sl 1 P-wise) to end.
Rnd 21: (K3, YO, K3, YO, K3, Sl 1 P-wise) to end. 84 sts.
Rnd 23: (K11, Sl 1 P-wise) to end.
Rnd 25: (K3, YO, K5, YO, K3, Sl 1 P-wise) to end. 98 sts.
Rnd 27: (K13, Sl 1 P-wise) to end.
Rnd 29: (YO, K3, YO, K7, YO, K3, YO, Sl 1 P-wise, PM) to end. 126 sts.

Rnd 31: (P1, K15, P1, K1, SM) 6 times, P1, K15, P1, KFB, SM. 1 st inc, 127 sts.
The extra st just created at the end of Rnd 31 allows the Seed St pattern to continue seamlessly from rnd to rnd. You may add a M to separate this extra st from the 7th rep on Rnd 32.
Rnd 32: (K17, P1, SM) to last st, K1.
Rnd 33: (P1, YO, K3, YO, K9, YO, K3, YO, P1, K1, SM) to last st, P1. 155 sts.
Rnd 34: (K1, P1, K17, P1, K1, P1, SM) to last st, K1.
Rnd 35: (P1, K1, YO, K17, YO, K1, P1, K1, SM) to last st, P1. 169 sts.
Rnd 36: (K1, P1, K19, P1, K1, P1, SM) to last st, K1.
Rnd 37: *P1, K1, P1, YO, K3, YO, SSK, K7, K2tog, YO, K3, YO, (P1, K1) twice, SM; rep from * to last st, P1. 183 sts.
Rnd 38, size 11.5" only: *(K1, P1) twice, K17, (P1, K1) twice, P1, SM; rep from * to last st, K1. Size 10.25" omit Rnds 38-41.
Rnd 39, size 11.5" only: *(P1, K1) twice, YO, K17, YO, (K1, P1) twice, K1, SM; rep from * to last st, P1. 197 sts.
Rnd 40, size 11.5" only: *(K1, P1) twice, K19, (P1, K1) twice, P1, SM; rep from * to last st, K1.
Rnd 41, size 11.5" only: *(P1, K1) twice, P1, YO, K3, YO, SSK, K7, K2tog, YO, K3, YO, (P1, K1) 3 times, SM; rep from * to last st, P1. 211 sts.
Rnd 42: *(K1, P1) 2 (3) times, K17, (P1, K1) 2 (3) times, P1, SM; rep from * to last st, K1.
Rnd 43: *(P1, K1) 2 (3) times, YO, K17, YO, (K1, P1) 2 (3) times, K1, SM; rep from * to last st, P1.
Rnd 44: *(K1, P1) 2 (3) times, K19, (P1, K1) 2 (3) times, P1, SM; rep from * to last st, K1.
Rnd 45: *(K1, P1) 2 (3) times, P1, YO, K3, YO, SSK, K2, CDD, K2, K2tog, YO, K3, YO, (P1, K1) 3 (4) times, SM; rep from * to last st, P1.
Rnd 46: *(K1, P1) 3 (4) times, K15, (P1, K1) 3 (4) times, P1, SM; rep from * to last st, K1.
Rnd 47: *(P1, K1) 3 (4) times, YO, K15, YO, (K1, P1) 3 (4) times, K1, SM; rep from * to last st, P1. 211 (239) sts.
Rnd 48: *(K1, P1) 3 (4) times, K17, (P1, K1) 3 (4) times, P1, SM; rep from * to last st, K1.
Rnd 49: *(P1, K1) 3 (4) times, P1, YO, K3, YO, SSK, K1, CDD, K1, K2tog, YO, K3, YO, (P1, K1) 4 (5) times, SM; rep from * to last st, P1.
Rnd 50: *(K1, P1) 4 (5) times, K13, (P1, K1) 4 (5) times, P1, SM; rep from * to last st, K1.
Rnd 51: *(P1, K1) 4 (5) times, YO, K13, YO, (K1, P1) 4 (5) times, K1, SM; rep from * to last st, P1. 225 (253) sts.
Rnd 52: *(K1, P1) 4 (5) times, K15, (P1, K1) 4 (5) times, P1, SM; rep from * to last st, K1.
Rnd 53: *(P1, K1) 4 (5) times, P1, YO, K5, CDD, K5, YO, (P1, K1) 5 (6) times, SM; rep from * to last st, P1.
Rnd 54: *(K1, P1) 5 (6) times, K11, (P1, K1) 5 (6) times, P1, SM; rep from * to last st, K1.
Rnd 55: *(P1, K1) 5 (6) times, YO, SSK, K7, K2tog, YO, (K1, P1) 5 (6) times, K1, SM; rep from * to last st, P1.
Rnd 56: *(K1, P1) 5 (6) times, K11, (P1, K1) 5 (6) times, P1, SM; rep from * to last st, K1.
Rnd 57: *(P1, K1) 5 (6) times, P1, YO, SSK, K1, CDD, K1, K2tog, YO, (P1, K1) 6 (7) times, SM; rep from * to last st, P1. 211 (239) sts.
Rnd 58: *(K1, P1) 6 (7) times, K5, (P1, K1) 6 (7) times, P1, SM; rep from * to last st, K1.

Rnd 59: *(P1, K1) 6 (7) times, YO, SSK, K1, K2tog, YO, (K1, P1) 6 (7) times, K1, SM; rep from * to last st, P1.

Rnd 60: *(K1, P1) 6 (7) times, K5, (P1, K1) 6 (7) times, P1, SM; rep from * to last st, K1.

Rnd 61: *(P1, K1) 6 (7) times, P1, Sk2p, (P1, K1) 7 (8) times, SM; rep from * to last st, P1. 197 (225) sts.

Rnd 62, size 11.5" only: (K1, P1) to last st, K1. Size 10.25" omit Rnds 62-63.

Rnd 63, size 11.5" only: (P1, K1) to last st, P1.

Rnd 64: (K1, P1) to last st, K1.

Rnd 65: *(P1, K1) to 4 sts before M, P1, SSSK, SM; rep from * to last st, P1. 183 (211) sts.

Rnd 66: (K1, P1) to last st, K1.

Rnd 67: (P1, K1) to last st, P1.

Rnd 68: *K3tog, (P1, K1) to 1 st before M, P1, SM; rep from * to last st, K1. 169 (197) sts.

Rnds 69-80: Rep Rnds 63-68 twice more. Size 10.25" omit Rnds 79-80. 127 (141) sts.

Rnd 81: (P1, K1) to last 3 sts, P1, K2tog. 126 (140) sts.
Continue to Ribbed Band.

Ribbed Band

Switch to smaller circular needles.
Work in 1x1 Rib for 13 rnds.
BO in pattern, using the Simply Stretchy Bind Off.

Finishing

Weave in ends, wash and block over a plate or circular object with a diameter of approximately 10 (11)" to achieve the beret shape.

Septafleur Chart

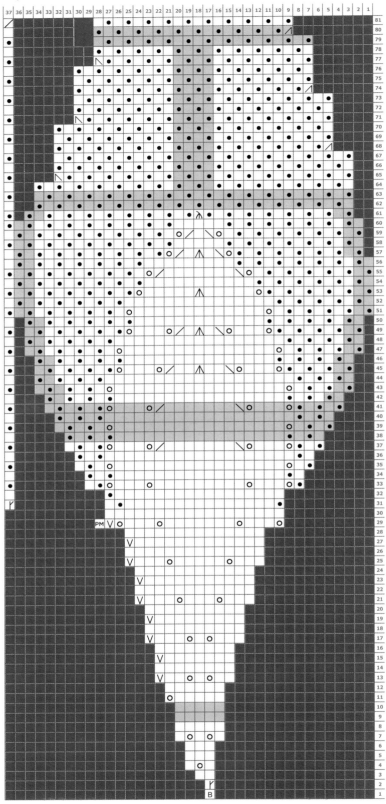

Legend

No Stitch
Placeholder - No stitch made.

B **knit tbl**
Knit stitch through back loop

kfb
Knit into the front and back of the stitch

knit
knit stitch

O **yo**
Yarn over

V **slip**
Slip stitch as if to purl, holding yarn in back

• **purl**
purl stitch

ssk
Slip one stitch as if to knit, slip another stitch as if to knit. Insert left-hand needle into front of these 2 stitches and knit them together

k2tog
Knit two stitches together as one stitch

Central Double Dec
Slip first and second stitches together as if to knit. Knit 1 stitch. Pass two slipped stitches over the knit stitch.

sl1 k2tog psso
slip 1, k2tog, pass slip stitch over k2tog

k3tog
Knit three stitches together as one

sssk
Slip 3 stitches as if to knit. Insert left-hand needle into front of these 3 stitches and knit them together

PM place marker

Size Large & Small

Size Large only

Note: Chart is worked 7 times per rnd. Read each chart row from right to left. On 7th rep of Rnd 31, KFB into last st, creating one extra st (represented by the single column at the left side of chart). This will allow you to work the Seed St pattern seamlessly from rnd to rnd. This extra st is dec in the final rnd of the pattern before the 1x1 Ribbed Band is knit.

Abbreviations							
		M	marker		stitch	TBL	through back loop
BO	bind off	M1	make one stitch	RH	right hand	TFL	through front loop
cn	cable needle	M1L	make one left-leaning	rnd(s)	round(s)	tog	together
CC	contrast color		stitch	RS	right side	W&T	wrap & turn (see
CDD	Centered double dec	M1R	make one right-lean-	Sk	skip		specific instructions
CO	cast on		ing stitch	Sk2p	sl 1, k2tog, pass		in pattern)
cont	continue	MC	main color		slipped stitch over	WE	work even
dec	decrease(es)	P	purl		k2tog: 2 sts dec	WS	wrong side
DPN(s)	double pointed	P2tog	purl 2 sts together	SKP	sl, k, psso: 1 st dec	WYIB	with yarn in back
	needle(s)	PM	place marker	SL	slip	WYIF	with yarn in front
EOR	every other row	PFB	purl into the front and	SM	slip marker	YO	yarn over
inc	increase		back of stitch	SSK	sl, sl, k these 2 sts tog		
K	knit	PSSO	pass slipped stitch	SSP	sl, sl, p these 2 sts tog		
K2tog	knit two sts together		over		tbl		
KFB	knit into the front and	PU	pick up	SSSK	sl, sl, sl, k these 3 sts		
	back of stitch	P-wise	purlwise		tog		
K-wise	knitwise	rep	repeat	St st	stockinette stitch		
LH	left hand	Rev St st	reverse stockinette	sts	stitch(es)		

Knit Picks yarn is both luxe and affordable—a seeming contradiction trounced! But it's not just about the pretty colors; we also care deeply about fiber quality and fair labor practices, leaving you with a gorgeously reliable product you'll turn to time and time again.

THIS COLLECTION FEATURES

Galileo
Sport Weight
50% Merino Wool, 50% Viscose from Bamboo

Alpaca Cloud Lace
Lace Weight
100% Baby Alpaca

Luminance
Lace Weight
100% Silk

Capretta
Fingering Weight
80% Fine Merino Wool, 10% Cashmere, 10% Nylon

Diadem Solid
Fingering Weight
50% Baby Alpaca, 50% Mulberry Silk

Capra
DK Weight
85% Merino Wools, 15% Cashmere

Gloss Fingering
Fingering Weight
70% Merino Wool, 30% Silk

Paragon
Sport Weight
50% Fine Merino Wool, 25% Baby Alpaca, 25% Mulberry Silk

Gloss DK
DK Weight
70% Merino Wool, 30% Silk

Reverie
Worsted Weight
80% Baby Alpaca, 20% Acrylic

Aloft
Lace Weight
72% Super Kid Mohair, 28% Silk

Alpaca Cloud Fingering
Fingering Weight
100% Superfine Alpaca

Andean Treasure
Sport Weight
100% Baby Alpaca

View these beautiful yarns and more at www.KnitPicks.com